Table of Contents

Introduction

It's two hours until sun-up. You silently slip into the still-dark woods. A veil of blue-white stars dances overhead; a sliver of new moon lights your way. You step carefully, not wishing to disturb the hush of wild things sleeping. You know this woods: the deer trails and fox burrows; each creek and hollow; every ridge and roosting tree.

OUTDOOR LIFE
THE SPORTSMAN'S AUTHORITY SINCE 1898 ®

Turkey
SEASON

Outdoor Life's EXPERTS SHARE THEIR TIPS, TECHNIQUES & CLASSIC STORIES

CREATIVE
PUBLISHING
international

MINNETONKA, MINNESOTA

Creative Publishing international, Inc.
5900 Green Oak Drive
Minnetonka, MN 55343
1-800-328-3895

President/CEO: David D. Murphy
Vice President/Editorial: Patricia K. Jacobsen
Vice President/Retail Sales & Marketing: Richard M. Miller

TURKEY SEASON

Executive Editor, Outdoor Group: Don Oster
Editorial Director: David R. Maas
Senior Editor and Project Leader: David L. Tieszen
Managing Editor: Jill Anderson
Creative Director: Brad Springer
Art Director: Russ Kuepper
Mac Designer: Joe Fahey
Photo Researcher: Angie Hartwell
Production Services Manager: Kim Gerber
Production Staff: Laura Hokkanen, Kay Swanson

Contributing Photographers: Jon Blumb, Toby Bridges, Gary W. Griffen, Donald M. Jones, Lance Krueger, Wyman Meinzer, Larry Mueller, Jeff Murray, Martin J. Tarby, Lovett Williams, Jim Zumbo

Contributing Illustrators: Stephen Fadden, Clay McGaughy, Arnold Roth, Michael Schumacher, Steve Stankiewicz

Cover Illustrator: cover illustration of "Oak Ridge Monarch" by Larry Zach, Zach Wildlife Art, tel.: 515-964-7872

Printed on American paper by: R. R. Donnelley & Sons Co.

10 9 8 7 6 5 4 3 2 1

Library of Congress Cataloging-in-Publication Data

Turkey Season : follow Outdoor life's experts into the turkey woods.
        p. cm.
    ISBN 0-86573-112-8 (softcover)
      1. Turkey hunting. I. Title: At head of title: Outdoor life.
    II. Creative Publishing International.

SK325.T8 T92 2000
779.2'4645--dc21

                                                                    99-049668

Standing quietly in the darkness, you raise the battered old owl hooter to your lips and softly blow the first "who-cooks-for-you?" call. A thunderous gobble cuts your hooting in two and you freeze, feeling the goose bumps roll over you like a wave. No more waiting for spring—it's here in a moment. Now it's just you and that old tom and the dawn of another turkey season.

Whether you're in the piney woods of Georgia, the eastern hardwoods of Pennsylvania or under a canopy of California live oaks, few sounds in the wild set a hunter's heart to racing faster than the gobble of a wise old longbeard at fly-down. The authors in this book—all turkey hunting fanatics—have captured that thrill in words and stories that anyone who plies the woods in spring or fall can appreciate. In *Turkey Season* you'll learn the tricks that have made them hunting's (and *Outdoor Life's*) best: Jim Zumbo, Mike Hanback, Bruce Brady, Michael Pearce, Lovett Williams, Ray Eye and the dean of all turkey hunters, Charlie Elliott. You'll also come to appreciate the special calling that draws us back each season to match wits with this grand old bird.

Follow that far-off gobble into the woods. Sit silently in the cool dawn with your back to a towering pine and strain your ears to catch the first flutter of hens coming to ground. You'll come away not only understanding what it means to really hunt, but why bringing a wild turkey to bag is one of hunting's great rewards.

Todd W. Smith
Editor-In-Chief
Outdoor Life

PROFILES OF THE BIG BIRDS

by Michael Pearce

WILD TURKEYS WERE NEARLY EXTINCT 60 YEARS AGO, BUT TODAY THEY'RE FOUND ACROSS THE UNITED STATES.

EVERY KINDERGARTNER worth his Big Chief note pad and cigar-size crayon knows that America historically had lots of wild turkeys. After all, the biggest of our gamebirds was the main course at the original Thanksgiving dinner. Turkey was also served at countless other, less glamorous meals, as well.

As "civilization" moved westward from the Atlantic through the prairies, people took their turkey dinners however they could get them. For roughly 250 years, wild turkeys were slaughtered the year-round—shot from roost trees and sometimes lured to bait-filled troughs where more than a dozen birds could be killed with a single shot. Because of unregulated killing, loss of habitat and possibly the introduction of disease from domesticated fowl, what once must have seemed like an inexhaustible supply of turkeys was nearly gone as recently as 60 years ago.

"Because no surveys were done, all we can do is estimate," said James Earl Kennamer, director of research and management for the National Wild Turkey Federation (NWTF). "We think that by the 1880s there were probably only about 30,000 wild turkeys left in the country. The birds that were left were in scattered remnant flocks in areas that were mostly inaccessible to humans. The turkey population basically stayed near that all-time low right on through the days of World War II."

Finally, wild turkeys began to benefit from sportsman-funded modern game management practices. "For the past several decades," Kennamer said, "state game departments have been reintroducing and introducing wild turkeys with great success. The birds are trapped—usually over bait with a drop or rocket net—and moved to a new area."

If the birds are from good stock and the habitat is right, it doesn't take long for them to take hold. According to Kennamer, traditional releases have included about a dozen hens and three or four gobblers. "They can be extremely fertile and successful," Kennamer said. "That small flock can grow to up around 400 turkeys in as little as five years if normal reproduction takes place."

The capability of producing like rabbits and being able to adapt to habitat once considered inferior for turkeys has made the comeback of the wild turkey the gem of wildlife management.

"Turkeys have no doubt done better than we ever hoped even a few years ago," Kennamer said. "We now estimate the nationwide population at 4 million turkeys. That's up a full million turkeys from the 1986 survey! We now have huntable wild turkey populations in 49 states." (Alaska is the exception.)

DISTRIBUTION

It's a true gift from Mother Nature that we have wild turkeys in nearly every region in the country where there are enough trees to hold a flock. Biologists recognize five separate subspecies of wild turkeys. One subspecies, the Goulds of extreme southern New Mexico and Arizona, is considered too threatened to allow a hunting season. The four other subspecies—Easterns, Floridas, Rio Grandes and Merriam's—are thriving and in huntable numbers. Though they have more in common than not, each subspecies has evolved to perfectly fit into the habitat it calls home.

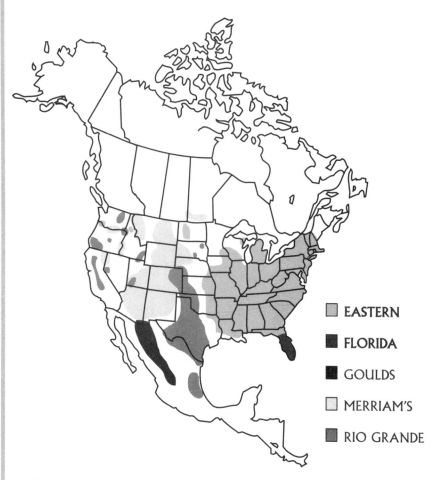

- ■ EASTERN
- ■ FLORIDA
- ■ GOULDS
- □ MERRIAM'S
- ■ RIO GRANDE

EASTERNS

Without question, the most numerous and widespread turkey subspecies in America is the Eastern. These birds range from the Florida Panhandle up into Maine and several Canadian provinces, and from the Atlantic coast to the eastern parts of Kansas, Oklahoma and Texas. Once thought of as a bird of big, unbroken woodlands, Easterns have adapted well to the small pockets of hardwoods in the Midwest. In fact, some of the densest turkey populations in the country come where crop fields and woodlands are intermixed.

Their range proves that Easterns are very adaptable to weather ranging from the heat and heavy rains of the South to the cold and snows of Canada and the New England and northern Midwestern states.

Easterns are noted for having some of the longest, thickest beards of all turkeys. Though there is always some genetic variance, the tips of an Eastern's tail feathers as well as its back feathers are usually chocolate-colored.

FLORIDAS

Though it's sometimes debated, biologists recognize the turkeys of central and southern Florida as a separate subspecies. Appropriately called Floridas, or Osceolas, these birds inhabit the flat, often-swamp- filled woods of the region.

Adaptable Eastern turkeys are numerous and widespread, and are known for their chocolate-colored back and tail feathers and thick, long beards.

Looking remarkably like Eastern turkeys, Florida toms are slim of body but often long of spur. The least widespread of the four huntable subspecies, Florida turkeys are in great demand by hunters interested in taking the "grand slam" of all four subspecies of turkeys.

RIO GRANDES

As their name implies, Rio Grande turkeys

Florida, or Osceola, turkeys are often slender of body.

were originally from the plains states of Texas and Oklahoma. Their ability to survive in semi-arid conditions now has Rio Grandes gobbling in California, Oregon, Washington, Utah, Nevada and Kansas.

When asked to describe Rio Grandes in a single word, one biologist said, "Adaptable. If I could use two words, I'd say, 'Remarkably adaptable.'"

Biologists, landowners and sportsmen are constantly amazed at where Rio Grandes can thrive. It was once believed that the birds would only survive along major stretches of riparian habitat, such as heavily timbered river bottoms. Now Rios are thriving along tiny, dry tributaries and even in shelterbelts around farmsteads in Kansas and Oklahoma.

Rio Grande turkeys thrive in semi-arid habitat, often sport smaller beards than Eastern birds and have beige to tan tail feather tips.

Equally adept at growing fat in both native prairies and lush crop fields, it appears that an abundance of rainfall may be the Rio Grande's main limiting factor. Surveys show that Rios do best in areas with less than 30 inches of annual rainfall.

Merriam's are beautiful with white tail feather tips.

Rio Grandes often sport smaller, thinner beards than Eastern and Florida birds, and they carry tail feathers that range from beige to tan at the tips.

MERRIAM'S

America's true mountain turkeys, Merriam's have been transplanted from their native New Mexico and Arizona throughout much of the Rockies and the Black Hills of South Dakota. They're also at home in many river drainages across the high plains and as far east as central Nebraska.

Merriam's weather the cold and snow the same way the mule deer they share their range with do. During the summer, Merriam's can be found as high as 12,000 feet, but winter migrations of 40 to 50 miles to agricultural areas aren't uncommon.

With beards that are more similar to those of Rios than Easterns, Merriam's are the hands-down favorite as the prettiest turkey in the nation. Many Merriam's sport tail and back feathers that are brilliantly white-tipped.

HYBRIDS

Given a chance, different subspecies of wild turkeys will readily interbreed or will breed with feral birds. The offspring of such breedings are fertile.

Such interbreeding is common where two subspecies' ranges come together. For example, Rio Grande and Eastern crosses are so common in central Kansas that biologists feel there are few, if any, purebred Rio Grandes left in the area. On some occasions, Kansas has intentionally encouraged such interbreeding by introducing a few Eastern toms into a stagnated flock of Rio Grandes. Most times such hybridization has led to a turkey population explosion.

TURKEY TRIVIA

- Day length is the main element that triggers springtime mating behavior. Receptors in the turkeys' eyes get the hormones going that start gobblers gobbling and trigger the mating process in the hens. Weather can, however, have minor effects on gobbling and mating intensity.

- Hen turkeys can be a little more promiscuous than they need be. "A hen only needs to mate one time to fertilize her entire clutch of eggs," said the NWTF's James Earl Kennamer. "Sperm can remain alive in a hen's system for up to a month, but it's not uncommon for a hen to mate with several different toms. Depending on the circumstances, it's very possible that a brood of chicks could be from several different gobblers."

- The average clutch consists of 10 to 12 eggs, though much larger clutches have been recorded. If a hen's nest is destroyed before the eggs hatch, she'll usually try to re-nest. Kennamer cited examples of radio-collared hens trying four times before they pulled off a successful hatch. Such hatches sometimes don't occur until as late as early September.

- It's estimated that 50 to 70 percent of turkey mortality occurs with chicks younger than six weeks of age. "Both natural predation and the weather can take a big toll," Kennamer said. "Until turkeys are old enough to fly into a tree or brush, they're very vulnerable and are preyed upon by nearly every predator in the woods."

I'VE FOUND TURKEYS FULL OF WASPS, STINKBUGS AND POISON IVY SEEDS.

- What do turkeys eat? It would be easier to list what they don't eat. Some parts of their diet would shock some people. "A lot of what turkeys eat we sure wouldn't eat," Kennamer said. "I've found turkeys full of wasps, stinkbugs and poison ivy seeds. They'll eat about anything they can get in their beaks. That includes little snakes and lizards." In addition, wild turkeys, like most gamebirds, feed heavily on wild marijuana seeds where available.

- Along with natural mast and planted grains, insects make up an important part of a turkey's diet. "Turkeys feed very heavily on insects," Kennamer said. "They'll even dig down and find bugs in the winter. Grasshoppers play a very, very important part in the life cycle of turkeys in the summer. Both young and old birds can get a lot of their moisture and protein in one meal by eating grasshoppers."

- Most turkeys are homebodies that are born, live and die within a few square miles. There have been recorded cases, however, in which a bird has wandered for dozens of miles. Sometimes turkeys settle into a new territory and sometimes they turn around and march right back from where they originally came.

- Beard length and body weight have little to do with a gobbler's age or dominance. Genetics and living conditions are the key factors. "We have mature Easterns in the deep South that only weigh 16 to 17 pounds," Kennamer said. "Then again we have Merriam's up in the grain belt of the Dakotas that weigh far more because of their diet."

- Though spur length is the easiest way to age a gobbler, it's no surefire indication that the long-spurred gobbler you've just bagged is the dominant bird in the area. Like all animals, turkeys can eventually grow past their prime and be replaced by younger birds.

- Most biologists don't believe that one subspecies of turkey is inherently more challenging to hunt than another. "There's no question that most people feel that Eastern turkeys are tougher than Rio Grandes or Merriam's," Kennamer said. "But I think it's important to note that in most places Easterns have been hunted harder and for a lot more years. There's been a lot of genetic selecting taking place, and the birds do react differently when they've been pressured—no matter what the subspecies."

Kennamer relates a hunt on a Colorado ranch nearly a decade ago. "The Merriam's there had never been called to or hunted by people," he said, "and they were very gullible. We called one right up to within 15 steps of a man wearing a white T-shirt. Then the rancher started leasing hunting rights, and the turkeys started getting pressured hard. Within a year he had turkeys that would shut up when they'd hear a box call."

CASING TOM'S PLACE

by Kathy Etling

CALLING AND PATIENCE CAN BE WORTHLESS
WEAPONS WITHOUT SOME PRE-SEASON SCOUTING.
KEEP IN MIND A FEW CLUES, AND YOU CAN STAY
A STEP AHEAD OF CAGEY LONGBEARDS.

I HUNTED FOUR SEASONS before I killed my first gobbler.
Four long springs, during which I wavered between hope and despair
and endured a heaping dose of frustration. I often wondered what I
was doing in the woods, a typical feeling for a beginning turkey
hunter and a thought not uncommon even for a veteran.

So even though I was a passable caller with plenty of patience, the
only reason I killed my first gobbler was because after four years of
hunting the same area, I knew the land well enough to predict the
turkeys' movements. During the early years of my turkey hunting
career, I never scouted before the season. And I wasn't clever enough

to see how the lay of the land could affect the gobblers' actions. I only knew that no matter what I did, it was always wrong.

But when a tom answered me eagerly on opening day that fourth spring, I knew better than to count on him coming to me. Instead, I remembered all of the other gobblers I'd thought were coming but had never showed. I remembered how they'd be in front of me one minute, then behind me the next. And I remembered thinking that they must have favorite travel routes from one spot to the next.

Then it dawned on me. In my mind's eye I suddenly saw the best place for turkeys to cross the narrow field between these spots. I remembered a neck of trees that extended almost completely across this field, trees that grew in a slight depression area, making a perfect travel lane for a cagey bird. A gobbler could cross that field without leaving cover.

So I decided to act on this hunch. I slipped closer to the spot where the shallow swale entered the woods on my side of the field. I set up in a spot where, if the gobbler appeared where I thought he might, he'd be close enough to shoot.

I called, and the tom thundered a reply. He was headed my way. I got the old Stevens single-shot 20-gauge up on my knees and waited.

Moments later, not one but three big gobblers sauntered into view. Just as I'd suspected, they were using the depression as a corridor. All of the birds looked huge, but the last one's beard was spectacular. It nearly dragged on the ground as he walked.

My mouth went dry as I waited for the three toms to move into range. But what I hadn't noticed was the small, dirt hillock between me and the birds. As they moved behind it, all I could see were three bright-red heads, bobbing one after another like ducks in a shooting gallery.

I lined up my best shot on what I thought was the largest bird, and bang! The woods erupted as turkeys seemed to take off in every direction. My heart sank. With only the bird's head to shoot at, I thought I might have missed. But when I looked over the mound, my first gobbler lay sprawled on the other side. At that moment I was the happiest hunter alive. And to this day, that first bird had the longest beard of any gobbler I've ever taken—12½ inches long.

It took four long seasons for one important fact to finally sink in: Scouting makes you a better turkey hunter. Choosing the right place to hunt and studying it well are prerequisites to consistently successful turkey hunting. And although turkeys don't leave the same kinds of semi-permanent sign that whitetail deer do—sign that can last until the next season—they do leave clues you can use to your advantage. Knowing how to interpret these clues and how to work the landscape could put you on the fast track to spring gobbler success.

If I had really examined my area before killing that first gobbler I might have succeeded much sooner. Instead, I relied on calling and patience and expected the birds to cooperate. But turkey hunting rarely goes according to plan—unless that plan includes scouting. I didn't really call that first bird to me. I made it easy for him to come my way by guessing which route he would take. Often, that's all you need.

Your first step in scouting is deciding where to hunt. If you're just starting out, look at your state's harvest statistics for the previous spring and fall. They should tell you where most of the turkeys were killed. These figures can indicate a high population of birds, a high number of hunters or a combination of the two. Counties with the most public land will usually have the highest harvest but will also have the most hunters. Look for places where access to public land is limited or difficult to travel to. Walk-in areas, where no vehicles are allowed, can also be prime targets.

If you narrow your choices down early enough—say, by January, February or early March—you can use your vehicle to pre-scout from the road. This is especially effective in agricultural areas. Often, large flocks of turkeys will feed on waste grains on cold, sunny days. This can give you an idea of how many turkeys an area holds.

Flocks break up for the mating season at various times, again depending on latitude. It may be as soon as early February in the South, and as much as six to eight weeks later in Northern states. Once flock breakup takes place, head into the woods early in the morning and listen. Gobbling will begin after break-up and will peak at various times depending on latitude and the weather. At this time toms are battling for territories and dominance—the right to breed freely with no interference. The birds will be vocal, and this is when you'll be able to get the best idea of how many gobblers are actually using an area.

Later, gobbling activity seems to diminish. The dominant tom will still sound off, but birds he's vanquished won't gobble much at all.

Still, just before the season opens is an ideal time to make one or two additional scouting trips. And if you didn't walk before, be prepared to walk now.

Get out early, well before light, and be at the spot where you plan to start hunting on opening morning. The first gobbles you hear will come from birds on the roost. Make a mental note of their general location. If you can get a good topographical map of the area, do so. On it, mark the places where you think birds might be roosting. And resist the urge to call. A gobbler tricked once is a gobbler that's harder to call later.

Turkeys will usually fly down from their roost just after first light. You might hear their wings flapping or perhaps just notice that the gobbles sound different. Note on a map, if possible, where they fly down and try to determine where they go once they're on the ground.

Sometimes a gobbler will get together with hens right off the roost.

Other times, a gobbler may go to a favorite area, or strutting ground, where he can see and be seen, a place where the hens know they can find him. Often, he may service hens after he flies down, then head for a strutting area later. By carefully listening for several mornings you might be able to foil his game plan with one of your own. Getting between the gobbler and where he wants to go—to the hens—is always an effective strategy. Heading him off at the strutting area will work, too. But both of these plans can be easier said than done.

Gobbling may stop completely around 9 or 10 a.m. and may resume later when the tom has worked his way through all of the willing hens. This is a good time to get acquainted with the area's terrain. Take your map with you.

Head for areas where you think gobblers were roosting. An undisturbed bird often roosts in the same general area year-round. Finding wing feathers scattered about or droppings under trees are both good clues. According to Larry Vangilder, turkey biologist for the Missouri Department of Conservation, a gobbler's primary wing feathers measure from 18¾ to 2½ inches in length, and a hen's vary from 15 to 17¼ inches. Like anything else in nature, however, there will be some overlap. But if you find several fresh wing feathers in an area—long wing feathers—you can bet gobblers have roosted there. In the spring, you can also identify a gobbler's wing feathers because they're squared off at the tips.

As for roosts, it's hard to pinpoint which trees turkeys prefer. In an area with many small trees, turkeys may choose the tallest, sturdiest trees they can find. In many parts of the country, turkeys seem to prefer pines and oaks, especially those with at least one stout branch growing parallel to the ground and with plenty of headroom above. Unfortunately, in some places that covers most of the trees in the woods. In hilly terrain, turkeys often prefer to roost in trees growing about halfway to two-thirds up a ridgeline.

Droppings remain one of the best clues to a turkey's presence and sexual identity. Those that form a "J" almost always belong to a gobbler; those that form a squiggle belong to a hen. You'll find droppings at roost areas. However, during all of the years I've hunted turkeys, I've only found one tree with a tremendous pile of droppings at its base. More often than not, turkeys choose roost areas rather than a specific tree, and droppings will be scattered.

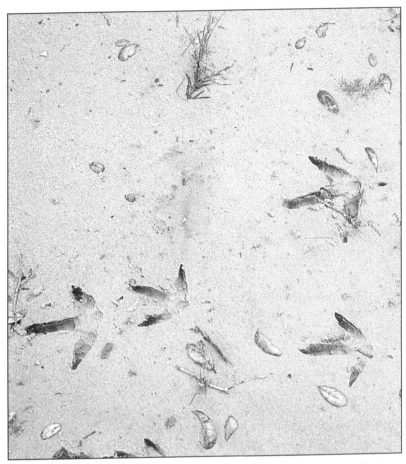

The track of a mature Eastern-strain gobbler will measure 4 ½ inches long or longer. When scouting, keep your eyes on the ground, especially in sandy, muddy areas.

You may also find droppings along the paths turkeys take. Along these pathways, look for strutting grounds. In my experience, turkeys seem to like strutting on a hard surface, one that's fairly free of tangled undergrowth.

While you're scouting your area, keep your eyes on the ground. You're not only looking for droppings and wing feathers, you're looking for tracks and breast feathers, two other important signs of gobbler activity. Also look for tracks in mud or dust. According to Vangilder, any Eastern-strain-turkey track that measures 4½ inches or more from the front of the toe to the back of the heel belongs to a mature gobbler.

Parallel drag marks in the dust or mud are a dead giveaway to a gobbler's strutting ground. These marks indicate where the gobbler's wing tips scraped the ground while he was displaying. Drag marks are difficult to spot. They look like someone took a stick and pulled it through the dirt.

DROPPINGS REMAIN
ONE OF THE
BEST CLUES
TO A TURKEY'S
PRESENCE
AND
SEXUAL IDENTITY.

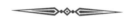

Also look for luminous feathers in striking shades of bronze, copper, green, pink and purple tipped with black. These feathers are from a gobbler's breast. They're another tip-off to a favored strutting zone. A hen's breast feathers are tipped with brown.

Scratchings, small patches of exposed ground where turkeys kicked away leaves or other debris while feeding, are another tip-off. Old scratchings will have litter in their centers, and their edges will be flat. Newer ones will have clean centers with leaves or other debris piled up at the rear edge. Scratchings show you where turkeys have been feeding, and an area with lots of fresh ones is a good place to set up and call. You can even track turkeys using their scratchings.

The turkeys kick the leaves behind them, so the side of a scratching with no debris is the direction in which a turkey is headed.

Make your area's terrain work for you, too. Try to figure out the easiest ways for a gobbler to get from one spot to another. In an area of steep hills and narrow valleys, something as insignificant as a slight saddle on a ridgetop might make a gobbler cross there. In rolling farmland, a favorite crossing might be a depression in a field or a dip where he'll be out of sight. Turkeys use fencerows, and birds often travel along field edges. If you spot turkeys in any of these places more than a few times, it's a good bet you've stumbled across one of their regular routes. A spot like this makes a terrific ambush location in the late morning after gobbling dies down.

Scouting for turkeys can work no matter where you hunt these wary birds. It's a simple matter of knowing what you're looking for and then putting it all together. And if you do your job correctly, you won't have to wait four long years to bag your first gobbler. Waiting is the hardest part.

TURKEY SCOUTING SABOTAGE

by Shirley Grenoble

WITH ALL OF THE HOOTING, GOBBLING AND
YELPING GOING ON IN PRE-SEASON, IT'S NO WONDER
THAT THE BIRDS HAVE SHUT UP COME THE OPENER.
THIS YEAR, WHY NOT TRY SOMETHING DIFFERENT?
SIMPLY LOOK, LISTEN, LOCATE AND SCORE!

FOR EVERY HUNTER who bags a gobbler this spring, five
others will end their seasons birdless. Two of the five will have
sabotaged their hunts themselves, most of them without realizing it,
and the third may well have been the unwitting victim of someone
else's sabotage tactics.

The "unlucky" hunters will blame hunter pressure, birds that wouldn't gobble, birds that hung up, gobblers that had hens with them and so on. Few will attribute the difficult behavior of the birds to what is so often the reason for their actions: the gobblers' awareness of and adaptation to the fact that the enemy has invaded their territory and learned their language.

Thousands of hopeful gobbler hunters annually invade the woods weeks before the season opens and work hard teaching gobblers to be balky, uncooperative and closemouthed. These hunters believe that they are doing pre-season scouting, but they are actually doing everything but.

Pre-season scouting is possibly the most important preparation a turkey hunter can make to ensure a successful season. Before the season, locating birds, zeroing in on the habits and patterns of a gobbler or two, and studying the terrain to be hunted will all give a hunter an edge over the more lackadaisical hunters who perhaps had neither the time nor the inclination to prepare properly for the hunt.

Unfortunately, pre-season scouters spend little time doing any of these things. The six- to eight-week period prior to the season opener that wise hunters should be using to their advantage has evolved into a kind of gunless mini-season in which thousands of hunters parade openly in the woods and educate the birds. They do this by calling gobblers in with gobble imitations and owl hoots every morning and evening from the same places along the road, and by spooking gobblers right and left and interrupting the breeding cycles. By the time opening day arrives, hunters may indeed know where some gobblers are hanging out, but the gobblers have learned a thing or two as well.

Though those who hunt gobblers tend to think of the birds as "smart," turkeys have neither the intelligence nor the reasoning powers of humans. They learn by association—by what is called conditioning. When the same things happen repeatedly, they learn how to react, and they adapt to survive.

In heavily hunted states—Pennsylvania, for instance, has 350,000 spring hunters—it's safe to say that at least half of the hunters will scout before the season. For many, it will be the first outing after a winter of cabin fever. When they hear that first gobble, the exhilaration and excitement they feel makes it almost impossible for them to resist the temptation to see whether they can lure the bird in. Watching the bird approach and perhaps strut, its iridescent feathers shining in the sun and its raucous, wild gobbling raising goose pimples along the caller's spine, is so addictive and thrilling that the hunter can't wait to try it again. It's sort of like sex; you can't say that you'll try it only once.

Perhaps the hunter wants to take pictures or film a video. Perhaps he's trying to show a newcomer just what the sport is all about. And isn't this the perfect time to practice your calling skills to see whether you really are good enough to call birds in?

There are many reasons why pre-season scouters spend their time calling birds in rather than just scouting for them. But there is a price to be paid for this pre-season foolishness, and the hunter generally begins reaping what he has sowed just about the time he can head into the woods with a gun.

You can bet the family farm that one of two things is going to happen with gobblers that are lured in to a hunter before the season. The first is that the gobbler will respond to the calling and come in, perhaps rather speedily. Gobblers in the early spring are ready to breed before hens are, and a sexy-sounding hen calling from afar may put a gobbler into high gear quickly. The hunter will sometimes be so well-camouflaged that the bird will approach within yards, clucking and perhaps even gobbling and strutting, but looking for that hen. After a bit, when no hen shows up, the gobbler will walk away. The hunter will congratulate himself on having called the gobbler in without spooking the bird, and he'll say to himself, "He won't be hard to handle when the season opens."

Perhaps one incident such as this will not bother a bird. But in high-pressure areas, such as farmlands or even mountainous country where there are plenty of access roads and trails and scores of hunters stumbling around on a daily basis, chances are slight indeed that this will be an isolated occurrence. In these areas, where hunters begin the season knowing that every other hunter in the vicinity also knows the location of every bird, most gobblers will have been worked several times prior to the season.

A time or two of running to an area with hopes of romancing the sexy hen he heard calling, and then finding nothing, conditions a gobbler to the futility of chasing after any hens that don't roost with him.

You'll recognize this gobbler during the season. He'll be the one that responds lustily when you call but does not move an inch in your direction. Maybe he'll even walk away from you, gobbling as he goes. He's learned his lessons well. Even though there may be other explanations for his behavior—he really may have hens with him, for instance—chances are good that he's simply responding as he has been taught.

A second situation arises when the gobbler responds to pre-season calling and comes in, but this time sees the hunter and is spooked. Perhaps there is a flicker of movement, perhaps a shiny button glints, but whatever the reason, he is scared off. Again, if the gobbler is spooked by scouters a couple of times, he'll be conditioned to be exceptionally wary of the calls of any hen he cannot see.

This gobbler is the one that gobbles until he hears a hen call from a distance. Then, he shuts up! He may not gobble at all from the roost, or he may gobble a lot but never move in the direction from which the calls are coming.

Again, pre-season conditioning may not be the only reason for this standoffishness, but it ranks high as one of the possibilities.

The practice of roosting gobblers has always been a favorite way to locate birds. Gobblers going to roost at dusk often gobble a few times, or they can be stimulated into gobbling by a sharp noise, a barred or great horned owl's call or another gobble. Because of this, hunters begin weeks before the season and continue until the last day of the season to roost birds every evening.

Roosting is done mainly along either mountain roads, from which a hunter need walk but a short distance to the head of a hollow or some other listening point, or roads that wind through farm country. The scouter parks his vehicle at a wide spot, gets out, gives the barred owl cadence or shakes a gobbler tube, and listens for the answer from a gobbler on the roost.

Naturally, few hunters walk a mile or more back into the woods to listen for a gobbler. Who has time for that? It's easier to drive from place to place to see how many birds can be heard in one evening.

Some years ago, I was hunting with a well-known turkey hunter in New York's Allegany State Park. Every evening we drove from spot to spot to listen for roosting gobblers. This hunter had a battery-operated megaphone into which he would hoot or gobble. The sound reverberated for hundreds of yards over those steep mountains. I'm sure the gobblers thought that Super Owl had arrived.

Over the years, gobblers have adjusted to this unvarying routine. They no longer bother to answer the owl hoots and gobbler calls that echo from the same spots along the same roads at the same times every evening.

As a result, roosting has become such an ineffective way to locate gobblers at dusk that many turkey hunters no longer bother. It has become a time and energy-consuming endeavor that no longer tells them anything. At one time, if no gobbler answered at dusk, a hunter could be pretty sure that no bird was there, and he knew to hunt elsewhere in the morning. No more.

This locating process also goes on at dawn throughout the turkey

woods, and it, too, starts weeks before the season and continues until the last day. Many hunters will not commit themselves to hunting an area until they hear a gobbler sound off. So, the daily routine is to drive from place to place, stop to hoot or yelp, and listen for an answer. If they hear nothing, they drive on.

The problem, of course, is that nearly all of the hunters drive the same roads, stop at the same places and use the same calls. How do gobblers respond to this morning parade? Kelly Cooper, a champion caller and one of Pennsylvania's best turkey hunters, gives this example: "Last season, I was working a wise gobbler on a ridge. I'd circled around and come in on him from a direction I didn't think anyone else had tried. There was a road on top of the ridge, and I knew that hunters called from up there every morning and evening, so I was clucking and softly yelping at the bird from the steep sidehill below. And he was gobbling like crazy.

"I heard a Jeep glide to a stop up on the road, and apparently the bird did, too, because when the guy began pouring out some sweet-sounding cackles and yelps, that gobbler never peeped. When the hunter started the motor and drove away, the tom gobbled on his own before the sound of the vehicle had died away. It was as though there had been a time-out while the lazy hunter did his thing."

Calling birds in before the season, scaring or perplexing them on a daily basis, and assaulting them every morning and evening with hoots and gobbles from the same spots have made present-day gobblers into sophisticated, wary birds. Today's gobbler has adapted and adjusted in response to the foolishness of overanxious hunters. Hunters are now realizing that they must adapt their hunting methods to accommodate the gobbler's new set of ground rules.

If we know what pre-season scouting should not be, we must define what it should be. Proper pre-season scouting tactics fall into three categories. None requires calling birds in or otherwise spooking them, and each, when done correctly, gives the hunter a decided edge for success. The categories are locating sign, zeroing in on the habits of particular gobblers and hens, and learning the country the hunter intends to hunt.

In the early spring, which usually means late February in Pennsylvania, turkeys begin to leave the areas where they flocked together in the fall to wait out the winter. They split into smaller groups and begin to spread out. In this exodus to new territory, it is the hens, not the gobblers, that lead the way. The reproductive urges are beginning to be felt, and the hens instinctively search out those places best suited for breeding and nesting. The gobblers go with the hens—or, perhaps more accurately, follow them—and because of this, a scouter should look for turkey sign, not just gobbler sign.

In the spring, wherever there are hens, there will be gobblers. Hens nearly always nest on or near the edges of farm fields or clearings. This is a key clue for a scouter, and it is also one reason—the other being easy access—why farm country gets hunted so hard. Hens gravitate toward the farm fields. However, a field or clearing need not consist of acres of land for a hen to love it. A suitable clearing can be a small grassy spot on top of a mountain, a reclaimed strip-mining site, an old orchard, a grassy mountain trail or logging road and so on.

Gobblers, of course, prefer to strut in open areas, and the clearings are ideal. Because both gobblers and hens are attracted to openings, the pre-season scouter can do no better than to begin searching for the clear places in his hunting territory. Clearings aren't the only places to find gobblers, but they're about the best places to start looking.

Tracks, droppings, feathers, food and water sources, scratchings, dusting areas and roost trees all tell the hunter where turkeys are hanging out. Finding this sign, coupled with listening for gobbles from that location, is what scouters should be doing. Sneaking in to listening posts before daylight and creeping around to look for sign can both be done quietly, without the turkeys ever knowing that you are there.

I call this kind of scouting "surface scouting." In any block of hunting territory, surface scouting will tell the hunter the areas that turkeys are favoring. If he hasn't the time to do any further scouting, the hunter at least knows the most likely spots to try.

The second dimension to scouting—one that few scouters actually do, yet one that every scouter should—is to zero in on the habits of the hens in a particular area. Few things can be more beneficial than this kind of scouting. This is serious scouting, and the more hunting pressure an area gets, the more important this facet of scouting becomes.

Hens and gobblers go through a fairly predictable routine just about every morning. One gobbler will establish himself as the dominant bird among a few hens. He will defend "his territory" (though it is really a territory that the hens have chosen) against all other gobblers. Even though he may allow one or two lesser gobblers to hang around, he makes sure that the others understand their subordinate positions in the pecking order and do not breed his hens.

It is these lesser gobblers that sometimes respond to a hunter's calls during the early part of the season. They are trying to pick a hen that is outside the dominant bird's perimeter and get a little action while the ornery old fellow is too busy with his own harem to drive them off.

Within his territory, the gobbler has a favorite area for his strutting and breeding activities. This area is called a strut zone. It's a clear spot—perhaps the edge of a field or an area of open woods—where he feels safe. He can see predators from a long distance and, most important to him at this time, he can perform his mating displays unhindered by brush so that his hens will be able to see his strutting from far off and be properly impressed.

Each dawn, his habit is to gobble to let his hens know that he's awake and will meet them shortly at the chosen spot. Some gobblers and hens roost together, others roost 50 yards apart, and still others roost 500 yards apart. If the gobbler and his hens were separated the day before, they will all make their way back to the established area to roost, but they may have to vocalize a bit in the morning to find each other. Each gobbler-and-hens flock establishes its own patterns, and the smart scouter spends time discovering the daily patterns of a few gobblers and their hens.

If a gobbler has been toyed with and harassed before the season, he's learned to gobble with restraint. He'll gobble softly once or twice to alert the harem, and then he'll glide or walk to the strut area. The hens have learned to cluck softly and do little more.

The surface scouter may know that there is a gobbler somewhere on a ridge, and when he hears that first gobble or two, he'll set up and call. He'll wonder later what he did wrong—why the gobbler never called again. The serious scouter knows where the gobbler is going and how the hens talk to him. He is positioned in that area and sounding like one of the hens before the gobbler gets there.

Perhaps a particular gobbler roosts well away from his hens. It's a habit of many gobblers to roost high on a point and glide down in the morning to a low point along a field to meet the hens. More-casual hunters who hear birds in an area a time or two will sneak in before dawn, get camouflaged and set up near that point. When the gobbler thunders from the roost, the hunter calls skillfully. The hunter thinks that the gobbler is responding to the calls, but when the gobbler flies off the roost, he glides to the bottom of the mountain or walks straight away from the calling hunter, gobbling as he goes. No amount of calling or moving to set up in a new area will draw in that bird. The hunter is baffled, wondering what more he could have done to interest that bird.

Had that hunter done some serious scouting and known that this gobbler roosts well away from the hens, he could have circled around before daylight, spooked the hens off the roost without scaring the gobbler, and positioned himself in the direction the hens went; he then would have had the gobbler in the palm of his hand.

Serious scouting is pinpointing the travel patterns of a couple of gobblers and their hens without interfering with the birds in any way. Once you know the travel lanes, the preferred strutting areas and so on, you can plot a hunting strategy.

Kelly Cooper hunts gobblers in north-central Pennsylvania, one of the most pressured areas in the state. Here's what he said about serious pre-season scouting: "The most important thing you can do in pre-season scouting is to pin down the travel patterns of a couple of gobblers. More important than having a dozen birds located is to know in detail about a couple of birds.

"When I have some birds located, I'll home in on a couple that I want to hunt the first day or two," Cooper said. "A week or so before the season begins, I'll go back to the area every morning. I won't make a call or any other sound, but I'll get 150 to 200 yards from a particular bird. I'll listen to him gobble, decide from the sounds how many hens he has with him, and hear which way he comes off the roost and in which direction he goes. When I've done that for three or four days in a row, I'll be waiting in the proper direction when he comes off the limb that first morning. This gives me an advantage over guys who go in there blind the first days of the season."

The third facet of smart pre-season scouting is learning the terrain. Sometimes, it can be done when surface scouting for sign. Hunters who hunt the same areas each season won't have to bother with this at all.

But turkey hunters are a highly mobile group. Scores of turkey hunters travel from state to state and from region to region within a state. These hunters use what limited time they have for scouting to listen, roost and look for sign. Many hunts are botched because a hunter isn't familiar enough with the area to avoid trouble spots.

A SCOUTER
SHOULD LOOK FOR
TURKEY SIGN,
NOT JUST GOBBLER SIGN.

Inflamed by lust as he may be, there are certain places a gobbler just won't enter or cross, even to get to the sexiest-sounding hen he's ever heard. In the East, these barriers are things such as wide streams or rivers, huckleberry swamps, mountain laurel and rhododendron thickets, clear-cuts, barbed-wire fences, large stone walls, deep gullies and small rocky drop-offs. Every section of the country will have barriers native to its topography.

And, of course, every turkey hunter has had an experience with a gobbler that, contrary to all established rules, did cross a barrier to reach him. But for every gobbler that does cross, five others won't. Taking time to track down trouble spots before you have a gobbler thundering from the other side of one is simply the smart thing to do.

Several seasons ago in northeastern Pennsylvania, a buddy and I heard a bird gobble just before daylight. We set up on him and began calling from where we were. It turned into a classic standoff. He was interested—that was obvious from his excited gobbling—yet he wouldn't move toward us.

I'd known beforehand what the problem was, but I couldn't convince my companion. He'd been hunting turkeys for more than 20 years longer than I, he'd already bagged a gobbler that year, and he was a far superior caller. When he had strongly resisted my suggestion that we move closer to the bird before beginning to call, I had mistakenly yielded.

I felt that I had an advantage over my buddy in this instance because I knew the country better than he did and was sure that the gobbler would never come to us, despite the skillful calling. I knew that 50 yards in front of us was a deep gully choked with laurel. There was no way that gobbler was going to cross that maze.

Twice, I suggested that we skirt the gully and cross onto the sidehill with the gobbler. "It's too risky," my partner said both times. "We'll spook him for sure if we try it." The third time, I didn't ask: I simply announced that I was going and that he could come with me or stay behind.

"I know this country," I told him. "I know exactly where that bird is gobbling from and how to get around this gully." He reluctantly agreed to go with me.

It took a bit more than a half-hour to skirt the laurel and climb up the other side of the hollow. During that time, the bird never gobbled, and I was fearful that he'd lost interest.

Cautiously, we topped the bench after our 30-minute sneak. "Call once just to locate him again," I whispered. The answering gobble nearly floored us, and we dove for cover. Fortunately, I had not removed my headnet or gloves during our move, so I sat down in front of the nearest tree and raised my shotgun. My buddy dropped flat on the ground beside me.

In short order, that gobbler was in front of me, no doubt believing he'd convinced that coy hen to finally come to him. But all he got was an education that day because my magnum No. 6 shot splattered a sapling in front of him and the air all around him. I caught a last glimpse of him as he scooted up the sidehill 75 yards away.

When I am hunting strange country and have no opportunity to scout, I am careful to ask the guide or my host to explain any topographic features that could be problematic.

There is a choice time to scout once the season has begun, says Wayne Bailey, 50 years a turkey hunter and formerly a biologist with various game departments. "It is helpful to be in the woods during midday," said Bailey. "Gobblers that gobble in the middle of the day or in the late afternoon are usually more vulnerable birds. They are often subdominant birds that haven't been allowed to breed, or they are gobblers that for some reason have been without hens for a time and so are more likely to respond."

In many states, turkey hunting hours in the spring conclude at noon. In Pennsylvania the deadline is 11 A.M., with the hunter required to be out of the woods by noon. There is no restriction, however, on a hunter's returning to the woods in the afternoon—sans gun, of course—for a scouting trip.

Gobblers may not be gobbling on their own in the afternoon, so it may be necessary for the hunter to do some hen or crow calling or hawk whistling to get a bird started. But once a gobbler responds, the hunter will want to leave the bird alone and get out of the woods immediately, especially if the bird responds to a yelp.

Nationwide, the success rate for spring gobbler hunters is about 5 percent. That figure could be doubled, I believe, if hunters didn't spend the weeks before the season so vividly advertising their presence and intentions to the quarry.

Ideally, pre-season is the time to creep silently into one's chosen haunts to listen and look. Educating birds before the season to be suspicious of calls that come from a distance puts a crimp in the sport for everyone. It's a tough enough sport to start with. Why deliberately make it tougher?

⟐

CALLS
THAT
COLLECT

by Lovett Williams

THE WILD TURKEY HAS 30 DISTINCT CALLS,
BUT YOU ONLY NEED TWO
IN THE SPRING TO MAKE HIM PAY.

WHEN I WAS 15, the wild turkey was a mystery to me, a ghost of the deep Florida swamp. So when I heard a man at the hardware store tell the clerk that he'd just shot his last two "high brass" turkey shells, I knew I'd found what I was looking for: a real turkey hunter.

I came close and told the stranger that there were turkeys where I hunted squirrels, that I'd found their sign but had seen only two birds—both at a distance. "What do I need to do," I asked him, "to kill a turkey?" His grin made his answer seem a little unkind. "All you have to do is get close enough to shoot one."

"And just how am I supposed to get close enough?"

"Just call 'em to you," he replied, then left before I could ask another question.

That seemed a little terse, but there were few turkeys in the late 1940s and even fewer turkey hunters—and those who knew a lot about the birds tended to keep it to themselves. I wasn't convinced that turkeys could really be called up, but I bought a $6 cedar yelper anyway.

I did manage to kill a few turkeys during the next three years, but not by calling them: I got them by just waiting all day wherever they had been the day before. My success was based almost entirely on luck. Then late one afternoon I was waiting in the swamp, listening to hoot owls and hermit thrushes and straining my ears for wingbeats, when I heard the sound of a lone hound dog in the distance. As I listened, trying to decipher its direction, the sound gradually began to resemble my Lynch yelper. Could it be . . . ?

I chalked up and scraped a few notes. Every time I yelped, so did the turkey, or dog, or whatever it was. My indelicate yelping drew the faraway sound toward me, and in less time that it takes to tell you about it, I was hauling a young gobbler out of the woods. I knew then that I should have gotten into calling sooner and that I was going to really learn to call turkeys.

Well, I did—or at least I think I did. I've been studying turkey calls for 28 years now and have even managed to make a living at it—by studying them and by hunting them. Some of the things I'm about to say may surprise you—they may even strike you as ridiculous—but I'm willing to take that chance. I'm not basing my ideas on conventional wisdom; I'm basing them on observation in the field, both as a hunter and as a scientist. And I know they work.

Calling has always been a part of turkey hunting, going back as far as the American Indians, and in recent years it has become the very essence of the sport. Today the yelper is almost as important as the gun.

Why? Because it's nearly impossible to sneak up on a wild turkey. Like any large and tasty prey species, they are vigilant in the extreme; any turkey stupid enough to be surprised by a clumsy human being was eaten long ago by something more agile. Despite their exceptional wariness, however, turkeys have one fatal

weakness: They are sadly vulnerable to imitated calling. Turkeys are gregarious by nature and use their voices to find one another in the woods, but the species has no innate defense against impostors because no predator, apart from man, has ever learned to impersonate them.

The wild turkey has at least 30 vocalizations—far more than any other bird studied. A few calls are used only by the nesting hen, others by the very young and three are used exclusively by spring gobblers—but most are used by all turkeys at one time or another. But turkeys are very social, very curious birds, and they will often investigate any turkey-like sound they hear. So you can learn 10 calls (see chart, p. 40)—plus your owl hoots, coyote whistles and crow calls—or you can cut to the chase.

CALL LOGIC

Despite what a lot of turkey pros will tell you, 90 percent of spring turkeys will respond to two relatively simple calls: the plain yelp and the lost yelp. Yelping will tempt turkeys of both genders and all age classes, and that includes old gobblers.

The plain yelp is the generic call of the wild turkey and is used year-round. It is usually given in a series of five to seven yelps, all at the same pitch and evenly spaced. The lost yelp, not surprisingly, is used by turkeys when they are separated from their flocks; it's similar to the plain yelp, except that it's louder and longer, usually in a run of at least 10 yelps, but sometimes with as many as 90 in a series.

Any type of yelping instrument will produce a perfectly good imitation of the real thing. And no amount of writing will tell you what that imitation sounds like. If you don't know, your first job is to get a cassette; there are plenty of them on the market. (When you do get one, you'll notice that a hen's lost yelp has a slightly faster cadence and a slightly higher pitch than a tom's. If you're going to learn only one lost yelp, remember who you're calling. Be a hen.)

The two yelps work especially well in hunting because they are the primary calls turkeys use to gather the flock. Have you ever heard a single gunshot in the woods but been uncertain of the direction it came from? There is no uncertainty when several shots are heard in succession. Repetitious yelping is designed by nature to make it easy for turkeys to track one another down.

The lost yelp is a logical choice for hunters because it can be heard over long distances. A lost bird is, by definition, a missing bird; the rest of the flock doesn't know where it is or even that it's missing. And a separated bird may wander for hours, or even days, yelping sporadically until it finds its way back to its flockmates.

But in fact, everything about a turkey's calling is logical, and hunters should take care to follow that logic. Like a hunter's signal shots, loud, repetitious calling is the most efficient way for turkeys to telegraph their position to their flock without being drowned out by extraneous noise. Such calls—lost yelps, cutting and cackling, to name a few—should be used when the hunter needs a long-distance call to locate turkeys.

Complex calls with multiple tones and/or several successive notes are used to reveal the calling turkey's location *so that others can join it*. The yelp and lost yelp are two "assembly calls" I've mentioned; gobbling, kee-keeing and cackling are others.

Soft calls such as plain purring and tree yelping are used at close range and are not intended to call turkeys to one another. Most cannot be heard outside the assembled flock and are generally of little value in calling turkeys. The same holds true for some of the close-range alarms: They're intended to communicate danger without attracting the attention of predators and are not very useful in calling distant birds, for obvious reasons.

But there is one important caveat to all of this. Anything that sounds like a turkey—except for the several predator alarms—may stir a bird's interest and bring him in. A prime example is the bizarre, "meaningless" strings of turkey sounds you sometimes hear at calling contests. So I wouldn't rule out using almost any sound or call if what you are doing isn't working and you feel like experimenting.

In general, though, you should respect the logic of turkey communication. An old tom close enough to hear a cluck is close enough to spot you, or damn near. The main purpose of a turkey's ears is to alert its eyes to danger, and if you've called him in that close, he's looking for you. The last thing you want to do is give a gobbler that last note that lets him pinpoint his would-be executioner.

IT AIN'T NECESSARILY SO

Turkey callers are often long on opinions. One old chestnut has it that you should call only infrequently. Think about that: Turkeys sometimes travel up to three miles per hour, so just 10 minutes of silence could permit a turkey to pass into and out of hearing range without having had the opportunity to hear you calling. When you call at least once per minute, that is unlikely to happen. Besides, turkeys themselves call long and often, and lost turkeys usually call at least once a minute for several minutes at a stretch. (Of course they may go for hours without yelping again. There's no rule, except that a lost bird doesn't play hard to get.)

Some hunters will tell you to call softly, although I'm not sure why. It sounds obvious, but the farther a call can be heard, the more likely it is that a turkey will hear it. Wild turkeys call loudly themselves and aren't offended if others do likewise. Call softly if you want to, but don't forget to call loudly as well.

What about "call-shy" birds? Well, a wise old hunter once told me that call shyness was a perfect explanation for one thing: why we spent all day in the woods and never saw a gobbler. There are many reasons why spring gobblers don't always come running when called, the main one being that according to the rules of turkey courtship, the receptive hen is supposed to come to the gobbler. Old toms will even ignore the calls of real hens. There's never been any research on wild turkeys becoming conditioned to artificial calls—and it may be a plausible theory. But then again, how would you ever know that a turkey didn't just have something better to do? It's certainly a bad bet from a natural selection perspective: A turkey that's "learned" to ignore calls is walking down a long and lonesome road.

Another thing to scratch from your list of worries is making an unturkey-like sound. Forget it. I've tested wild turkeys hundreds of times from sight-proof blinds (talking at them, whistling, tapping on a metal chair), and I can report that turkeys show remarkably little concern for foreign noises. But that shouldn't be surprising—many odd sounds are ringing through the woods almost constantly. The last thing on a turkey's "mind" is that some odd squeak was the work of an inept turkey hunter.

Then there's the fabled "love call" of the wild turkey hen. Sorry, it doesn't exist. If a hen could call a horny gobbler with a "come and get it" call, Cain and Abel would have eradicated the species. The turkey call most often labeled the love call is actually the plain yelp. The only true mating call of the wild turkey belongs to the spring gobbler himself and is intended to draw a hen to him when she's ready to mate. There *are* old gobblers around who will break those rules, however. And Lord bless 'em.

To master turkey hunting, all you need to do, as the parsimonious old hunter said, is get close enough to shoot one. "Just call 'em to you." And I don't mean that to sound unkind.

Yelpers like this push-pull call will bring in 90 percent of spring turkeys . . . if they're feeling curious.

TURKEY CALLS FOR HUNTERS

CALL: Plain yelp

MEANING: Many meanings

USE IN HUNTING: Call turkeys at moderate range. Main spring use: Primary call to use when working a responsive gobbler. Yelp to him every couple of minutes after you have his attention.

CALL: Lost yelp

MEANING: Assembly call of adult turkeys

USE IN HUNTING: Call scattered turkeys. Main spring use: Use at random to elicit a gobble at long range and to attract a distant gobbler; as gobbler approaches, change to plain yelp.

CALL: Single & double yelp

MEANING: Cautious assembly call heard most often when cover is heavy

USE IN HUNTING: Main spring use: When an approaching turkey is calling this way but you haven't spotted him yet. He will be reassured by the presence of another turkey and may eventually show himself.

CALL: Tree yelp

MEANING: Morning wake-up call

USE IN HUNTING: Main spring use: Elicit a response from roosting hen or jake. Use in likely roosting areas pre-dawn before loud calling is appropriate. Any response indicates a roost; a gobbler may be there as well and may gobble later.

CALL: Gobble

MEANING: Reveals gobbler's location to hens

USE IN HUNTING: Main spring use: To elicit gobbling or to call a dominant gobbler who is expecting competition. Can also be used pre-dawn as you would owl-hooting or crow-calling.

CALL: Cutting

MEANING: Elicits calling from other turkeys and reveals cutting bird's location

USE IN HUNTING: Main spring use: To attract lost or socially curious turkeys from a distance, or to elicit a cutting response from a flock or a shock gobble from a tom. A good call to use on hung-up gobblers, and at random to locate turkeys.

CALL: Cackle
MEANING: Meaning unknown; used only in flight
USE IN HUNTING: Main spring use: One of several loud calls that will elicit a shock gobble and may elicit an answer from a distant flock.

CALL: Kee-kee
MEANING: Lost call of young
USE IN HUNTING: Call young in fall.

CALL: Kee-kee-run
MEANING: Lost call of young
USE IN HUNTING: Main spring use: Call socially curious turkeys, especially jakes. Use from time to time at random intervals when not working a gobbler. Jakes follow adult gobblers and may respond, thereby tipping you off. Will also call young in fall.

CALL: Putt-purr
MEANING: Indicates mild concern & curiosity
USE IN HUNTING: Main spring use: To draw a nearby turkey even closer. May attract a hung-up gobbler.

CALL: Fighting rattle
MEANING: Anger call accompanying fighting
USE IN HUNTING: Main spring use: Can be used to get a responsive but hung-up gobbler's mind off sex. Will sometimes attract dominant gobblers who want to get into the fight and/or know of changes in hierarchy.

CALL: Plain cluck
MEANING: Means "Here I am, where are you?"
USE IN HUNTING: Use to elicit a response from an unseen but close-by turkey. Not very useful in spring hunting unless the gobbler is very close but unseen and the hunter is well-hidden and still. A cluck will reassure the bird that you (i.e., a hen) are there, but he will be looking hard and may spot you.

TURKEY CALLS FOR TURKEYS

CALL: Alarm putt
MEANING: Warns flock of suspected danger

CALL: Brood assembly yelp
MEANING: Used by hen to bring brood together

CALL: Chump & hum (drumming)
MEANING: Associated with strutting

CALL: Distress scream
MEANING: Indicates extreme alarm and distress

CALL: Feeding call
MEANING: A low-volume spacing call when feeding

CALL: Harsh predator alarm
MEANING: Used only by a startled turkey

CALL: Hatching yelp
MEANING: Used by hen in nest during hatching

CALL: High trill call
MEANING: Warns flock of suspected danger

CALL: Hush call
MEANING: Orders discontinuation of calling

CALL: Plain or soft purring
MEANING: A flock-spacing call when traveling

CALL: Poult whistling
MEANING: Signals distress

CALL:	Roost pitting
MEANING:	Warns roosting flock of suspected danger
CALL:	Singing alarm
MEANING:	Warns flock of suspected danger
CALL:	Spring jake yelp
MEANING:	Meaning unknown
CALL:	Threat cooing
MEANING:	A low-volume anger call preceding fighting
CALL:	Twittering alarm
MEANING:	Warns flock of suspected danger
CALL:	Whippoorwill call
MEANING:	A low-volume anger call preceding fighting
CALL:	Whit-whit
MEANING:	Meaning unknown

HOW TO TALK TURKEY

by John E. Phillips

TURKEY CALLING HAS COME A LONG WAY IN RECENT
TIMES, BUT WITH THE RIGHT CALLS, A LITTLE
KNOW-HOW AND PROPER PRACTICE, YOU CAN LURE
IN BOSS GOBBLERS JUST LIKE THE PROS.

TURKEY HUNTING is one of the fastest growing sports in the
United States today because more and more hunters have learned how
to use turkey calls. Through calling, the hunter actually communicates
with a turkey. He can pinpoint a gobbler's location, determine and
even change a tom's mood, and lure a gobbler in close or position him
for a close-range shot.

When you go one-on-one with a gobbler, you have to enter his world, think like he thinks and talk like he talks. In the movie "Patton," George C. Scott, who plays Patton, stands on a hill, watching the retreat of the tank corps of the famous German field marshal, Rommel, and screams, "I've read your book!"

Because Patton had read the book that Rommel had written on strategy, he was able to defeat the field marshal in Africa during World War II. To beat the smartest military strategist in the woods—the wild turkey—you not only have to know what a gobbler is thinking and understand where he wants to go, but you must carry on a deceptive conversation with him in an attempt to bring him close.

The Native Americans realized this when they tried to chase turkeys down and kill them with either rocks, spears or bows and arrows. With all of this effort, they must have said to themselves, "There's got to be a better way to take turkeys."

Early hunters noticed that during the spring of the year when a hen turkey started to call, often a gobbler would come to her. They determined that if they could reproduce the sounds of wild turkey hens, then instead of having to chase the gobblers, they could lure the birds to them.

The first turkey caller more than likely used his natural voice. As the sport of turkey calling evolved, woodsmen learned that they could scratch on wood, blow on properly held leaves and rub sticks and rocks together to make sounds to which gobblers would respond. But nowadays, learning to call turkeys in this manner could take years.

THE FIRST
TURKEY CALLER
MORE THAN LIKELY
USED HIS
NATURAL VOICE.

Luckily, there are a variety of commercially made turkey calls available to today's hunter that are both easy to use and productive. Of course, some are more difficult to master than others, but if you're willing to put in enough practice time, you might just find yourself sighting down your shotgun barrel at a strutting tom this spring.

THE BOX CALL

In the early 1900s, hunters discovered that they could whittle a box out of wood, attach a paddle to the end of it, and when they dragged the paddle across a surface on the box's wall, it could produce the sound of the wild turkey. During this time, several enterprising sportsmen began to make turkey calls to sell, and they taught other hunters how to use them.

You can reproduce a yelp with a box call by drawing the lid across one edge of the call with a single stroke.

One example of these early entrepreneurs was M.L. Lynch of

Homewood, Alabama—the founder of Lynch Game Calls—who traveled the South like a revival preacher, standing on street corners in front of drugstores and hardware stores and using his box calls to draw in crowds and sell his products. Lynch taught thousands of people how to call turkeys, and until the last 20 years, the box call was the device most frequently used to call in gobblers.

A thin-walled wooden box with a paddle lid attached to one end, the box call produces a sound when you draw the lid across the top of the box wall. The top of the wall and the lid are each chalked, and the different sounds created when these two chalked surfaces come into contact with one another mimic all of the calls of the wild turkey. A double-edged box (as opposed to those with only a single calling surface) encircled with a rubber band or bands allows you to shake the box back and forth to imitate a gobble. To reproduce a yelp with either a single or double-edged box, slide the lid across one edge of the box with a single, sweeping stroke. (When making a series of yelps, do not lift the paddle from the calling surface.) To make a cluck, place the lid on the top of the wall and pop it off with one quick stroke. A cutting sound comes from striking the paddle against the top of the wall several times in quick succession. To make a purr, draw the lid across the wall of the box lightly and slowly.

To produce the maximum amount of sound from a box, turn the box around so that the "front" is facing away from you (hinge toward you), and with your left hand (your right, if you are left-handed), hold the lid of the box perpendicular to the ground.

Then strike down on the lid (just the opposite of what you normally do) with the edge of the box.

THE PUSH-BUTTON BOX CALL

This simplest of all calls to use requires only that you push a peg with your finger to reproduce a hen call. With this call, you can make a clucking sound by simply tapping the end of the peg with the palm of your hand.

The push-button box call (cut away to show internal workings) only requires you to push a peg to reproduce a hen call. It's easy to use.

You can make yelps by pushing the peg three or four times in succession. You can cut by using the palm of your hand to pat the peg in rapid succession. Push the peg slowly and gently with your finger to make a purr.

The push-button call also can be taped to the forearm of your shotgun. In this way you can operate the call and hold your gun at the same time. This call is deadly on gobblers and is currently being used by many of the nation's leading turkey hunters.

Cup the slate's sound chamber in your hand, then move the striker across the surface to make a call.

THE SLATE CALL

With the original slate call, the hunter held in his hands a piece of slate and formed a sound chamber by cupping his hand around the slate. After first roughing up the surface of the call with a piece of fine sandpaper, the hunter would then scratch a wooden peg across the top of the slate to reproduce the sound of a wild turkey hen.

Forming the proper sound chamber to get a true-to-life turkey sound was often difficult, however; in later years the slate was encased in a box with a hole in the bottom that created the sound chamber. The peg is still used to scratch the top surface of the slate to produce a sound.

Today, many new products are being used to make "slate" calls besides slate. Plexiglass surfaces, plastic boxes and even aluminum are fast replacing slate rock and wood boxes.

Still, the same principles of operation apply, and to produce a sound, a striker is moved across the surface of the call. To cluck, you simply place the peg on the calling surface, holding it as you would a pencil with the point facing you, and sharply "pop" it toward you. Cut by making several fast clucks. To produce a yelp, make small circular motions on the surface, being sure not to remove the peg from the slate. For a purr, draw the striker slowly across the surface, applying just enough pressure to keep it skipping/skimming along.

THE MOUTH DIAPHRAGM CALL

In the late 1920s, a rabid dog was the catalyst that helped produce today's most popular call—the mouth diaphragm. Jim Radcliff Jr. of Andalusia, Alabama, was in New Orleans, Louisiana, being treated for rabies when he met a street entertainer who made bird calls with his mouth. Radcliff worked with the entertainer to modify and change the performer's diaphragm call—which was made of a small, hinged, horseshoe-shaped piece of lead across which a thin piece of latex rubber was stretched—to make it sound like the call of the wild turkey. This call was one of the first diaphragm turkey calls ever made.

Today the lead horseshoe of the diaphragm call has been replaced with lightweight aluminum, thinner pieces of latex are being used, and the body of the call is now covered with fabric or plastic tape. To use the diaphragm call, place it in the roof of your mouth (making sure it is not upside down or backward) and utilize your tongue to meter air over the latex rubber. The amount of air and the frequency with which the air is blown over the rubber reed(s) determines the kind of call that will result.

The diaphragm is the most difficult call to learn to use. You must seat the call properly in the roof of your mouth, position the tip of your tongue in the proper place on the reed and learn just how much air produces the different sounds of the wild turkey. The best way to learn to use the diaphragm call is to listen to an audio cassette. Put the call in the roof of your mouth, and then try to say the word "shoot" while blowing air over your tongue and vibrating the reed.

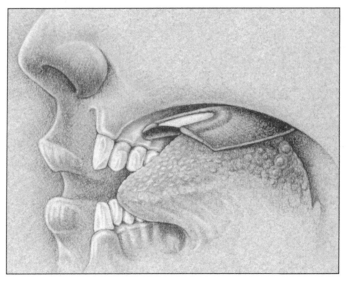

Press a diaphragm call into roof of your mouth with your tongue, then meter air over call's reed(s).

To make a cluck, put your lips together, blow out a short, sharp burst of air, and smack your lips at the same time. To cut on a diaphragm call, make a rapid series of clucks. By metering air over the diaphragm and dropping your jaw as the air passes over the rubber reed, you can make a yelp. To purr, which is the most difficult call to create on a diaphragm, make sure your lips are moist, then blow out while vibrating your tongue and lips up and down.

The pitch and the tone of the call made with a diaphragm are determined not only by the amount of air passed over the reed and the force with which the call is blown, but also by the number of latex reeds used in the call's frame and whether or not the reeds are split. The more reeds a call contains, often the deeper and more coarse, or raspy, the call sounds. Split reeds also make the calls raspier. Some diaphragm calls actually feature two frames taped together to make one call, which produces a different sound.

Veteran turkey hunters always carry an assortment of diaphragms into the woods. Often, toms respond best to variety. If one call doesn't work, try another.

OTHER CALLS

The tube call, or snuff can call, was first invented when hunters of yesteryear cut a hole in the bottom of a small snuff can, cut half of the lid away and stretched latex rubber over the opening in the lid, leaving a small slit opening between the rubber and the remaining lid through which air could pass. Blowing air over the rubber made a louder and often raspier call.

The wing-bone call originally was made from two bones in the turkey's wing. The bones were glued together to form a small pipe about six to seven inches in length and about a quarter-inch in diameter. To produce clucks and yelps, hunters sucked on the wing bone rather than blew air through it. Sucking small puffs of air through the wing-bone call produced a cluck, whereas longer, faster puff of air sucked through the call made a yelp.

TODAYS' TURKEY CALLS ARE MADE OF MANY DIFFERENT MATERIALS.

Today, turkey calls are made out of many different materials and come in a wide variety of types and shapes. Most turkey hunters agree that to effectively hunt and call the wild turkey, you must be able to use several different types of calls. On any given day, a gobbler will come to one call when he will not respond to another.

Remember, though, that a little calling goes a long way when you are talking turkey to a tom. You don't have to be a master of all types of calls to enjoy and be successful at the sport of turkey hunting. If you can produce a cluck and a yelp on any one of these calls, you can call in a gobbler.

SUPER SETUPS

by John E. Phillips

AFTER LOCATING A GOBBLER, REST EASY WITH ONE OF THESE FIVE SURE-FIRE TURKEY SETUPS.

FROM THE KEE-KEE to the gobbler yelp, to know the cadence and vocal inflections of turkey calling is to master a second language. As proof, check into the number of calling tapes and videos on the market today—enough to impress the most hard-boiled high school language teacher. Certainly accomplished turkey callers can hold conversations with entire flocks, wounding the pride of young jakes, enraging dominant hens and seductively luring boss toms into gun range. But many turkey hunters are not champion, or even accomplished, callers. What are their prospects for bagging a bird?

In reality, any turkey hunter can take a spring gobbler without making the kind of calls that excite a panel of judges. The trick is to first learn where a turkey is likely to go and then to set up along the turkey's preferred route of travel. In fact, many of the world's best turkey hunters agree that taking a stand in the right place contributes more to success than calling skill: Location and timing are the keys.

To know where to set up, however, you must understand what gobblers do not like to do. They do not like to cross ditches or fences. They do not like to fly or wade across water. Gobblers do not like to walk down hills, move through heavy cover or walk in areas where they have encountered hunters or other predators in the past. They do not like to journey into regions where a dominant tom threatens to beat them up. And they do not like to roam into clean woods when they hear hens calling but can't see those hens.

Of course, some turkeys will break these rules. But usually if you can set up in places where turkeys want to go rather than where they don't *like* to go, you're more than halfway toward bagging a bird. The accompanying illustrations and text detail five knockdown ways to set up on spring gobblers.

The first, what I call "The Magic Triangle," once put me in the position for the gobbler of a lifetime. I had been hunting for two days in the Mississippi Delta with Wil Primos and Ronnie Jolly, and I had only heard one turkey gobble. However, just at dark on the second day, the woods came alive with gobbling. Before daylight on the following morning, my friend Ronnie Strickland, Jolly and I went into the woods to find the gobblers. I took a stand about 100 yards from where the turkeys were roosting, and Strickland took a stand behind me and to my left. Jolly took a stand behind me to my right. I was the point of the triangle. Both Jolly and Strickland called and changed their calls periodically. The turkeys in front of us got so excited they double- and triple-gobbled. The birds flew down, and five jakes and one longbeard walked in front of me through some small saplings.

Strickland began to call aggressively to my left. As the birds moved to my left to find Strickland, Jolly called on my right and pulled the birds back to the right. The two callers kept the birds so confused they stayed in front of me for a long time, never quite figuring out where those two hens were that were doing the calling. I could have taken one of the jakes at any time, but the longbeard seemed to use the jakes as a shield. The setup worked perfectly, although I never was able to get a shot at the trophy bird.

Many turkey hunting experts agree that to take a gobbler, using the appropriate setups in known roosting areas far outweighs calling prowess.

Whatever the situation, it's imperative that you set up quickly. Often a sneaky gobbler will answer so close to you that there won't be time to look for the perfect stand site. Instead, you'll have to seat yourself immediately to avoid being seen by the gobbler. Clyde Jackson, an 80-year-old turkey hunter, offers some advice on this setup conundrum.

"Before I begin to call a gobbler, I look at the woods behind me," Jackson explains. "I also try to choose the best stand site close to me [before] the gobbler answers. Then rarely will a gobbler surprise me and force me to take a stand where he is likely to spot me."

THE MAGIC TRIANGLE

By using this unique setup, three hunters can confuse a gobbler and work the bird in close. This system also allows a trio of sportsmen to be a part of the hunt and enjoy the sport of calling and hunting turkeys together. Yes, turkey hunting can be a team effort (think of a basketball center and his two front court mates).

As the name implies, the Magic Triangle is a three-pointed strategy where one hunter becomes the top of the triangle while his two hunting companions set up behind him to form the triangle base. With the lead hunter resting against a tree about 100 yards from roosted turkeys, the other hunters set up about 30 yards behind him, flanking him on his left and right by about 20 yards. These hunters should conceal themselves from the oncoming gobbler.

The two hunters at the triangle base call simultaneously to create what sounds like squabbling hens. The gobbler flying down from the roost will be more than anxious to get to these hens. The lead hunter, with gun up in shooting position, will then intercept the tom on the bird's path to the hens.

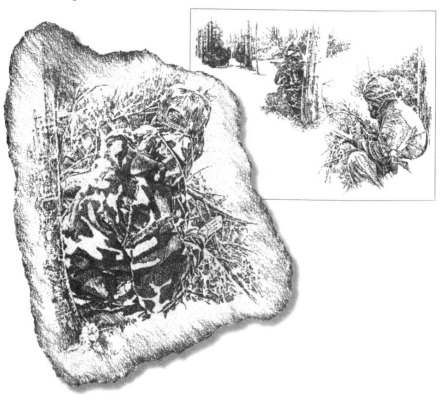

FIELD EDGES

Wide-open field turkeys often are the most difficult to take. If the turkey roosts on the edge of a field, flies down, lands in the field, spends all day in the field and then flies back to the roost at night, you may be able to take the bird by surprise early in the morning or about 10:30 A.M.

If you hunt the bird early, take a stand on the edge of the field about 75 to 100 yards away from where the gobbler is roosting. (Try to roost the tom the evening before you hunt to know exactly where the bird is.) While the woods are still dark, but when the field is becoming lighter with the onset of dawn, give a fly-down cackle. At the same time, flap your gloves against your pants leg to duplicate the sound of a hen flying down from the roost. Then begin the cutting cackle like an excited hen. Often, the tom will fly down earlier than usual just to get to the anxious hen.

Later in the morning, by 10 or 11, the sun will warm the field, and the birds will move to shaded areas. Make sure that some bushes are between you and the turkeys. Begin to call. If a dominant gobbler is in the flock, generally he will stay with the majority of the hens. But a subordinate gobbler often will break from the flock to investigate the seductive hen yelps.

WATER ROOSTS

In the spring when many river systems flood, turkeys like to roost over water in flooded timber regions, possibly for protection from predators. In this situation, when a gobbler calls from a tree, he wants to fly down over the water, touch down on dry land and meet his hens instantly—he doesn't want to fly 100 yards to find a hen. Before the season opens, scout the woods for a flooded basin. If the area is below a ridge, even better. This roosting area isn't necessarily a swamp, but a timber plot temporarily filled with water because of flooding from runoff or heavy spring rains. Then on opening day, search for a clear spot in the woods on the edge of flooded timber with a tree larger than your shoulders to set up against. Call very little. As the day breaks, have your shotgun resting on your knee, and be ready to make the shot. More than likely, when the turkey flies down, he will land within your shotgun range, searching for the hen that he thinks you are. However, the bird won't spend much time searching and will flee the area if he fails to see a hen.

DOUBLE TEAM

If turkeys are exposed to intense hunting pressure, a tom will often hang up when he hears calling. This tom knows that if a hen answers his gobbling, she should come to him as he displays. Although it is difficult to take a gobbler that hangs up, he can be had if two hunters double-team the bird. The shooter should set up 40 to 50 yards ahead of the caller between the bird and the caller. Then as the caller begins to call and the turkey responds to that calling, the shooter will intercept the gobbler before he hangs up and starts to strut and drum. This tactic is especially deadly on older longbeards late in the season.

HILLSIDE STRATEGY

Turkeys will walk uphill but usually not downhill in response to a call. Also, toms often strut and meet their hens on tops of hills. Take a stand on the opposite side of the hill from where you hear a turkey gobbling. Then begin to call to the bird. The gobbler will think that as soon as he reaches the top of the hill, the yelping hen will run up to meet him. Just as the tom peers over the top of the hill, he should be within gun range. You may only see the bird's head, however, so be sure to clearly identify your target before shooting.

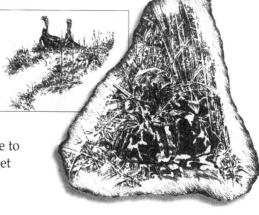

GOBBLER GANGS

by Ben Conger

SPRING GOBBLERS TRAVEL IN GROUPS.
IT'S A FACT. AND ONCE HUNTERS BEGIN TO
REALIZE THIS, THEY WILL START TAKING
MORE BIRDS FROM THE SAME AREA.

BUD WILLETTS, a 55-year-old veteran turkey hunter, was camo-clad and seated against an 18-inch-wide white pine, watching a harem of spring birds approach through the Vermont woods.

The harem's boss hen raced to Bud's decoy as soon as she came over the rise and spotted it. Six other hens followed. The lead hen halted with her beak three inches from that of the decoy and clucked sternly. The decoy ignored her.

Next, a strutting gobbler appeared, moving slowly, steadily. His tail was a full fan; his beard, a good eight inches long. His wing feathers scraped the ground. He would only pause when a second gobbler tried to pass him or attempted to fluff up in display. Either action would cause the leader to pirouette and glare. The offender would immediately deflate and skulk.

Five jakes brought up the rear. They pressed forward when the lead gobbler couldn't see them, and froze when he could.

The lesser hens had moved on and the boss hen was still clucking at the decoy when the lead gobblers stepped within shotgun range. Bud drew a bead on the strutting gobbler and downed him with a load of No. 6s.

At the shot, the hens ran a few steps and putted. The companion gobbler froze, as did the jakes. For a few seconds nothing moved. Then the companion gobbler rushed in and quickly stomped the fallen boss. When Bud stood to retrieve his prize, the birds fled.

During pre-season scouting and even during the early part of the spring season in many states, it is common to see a dozen or so turkeys together. And though turkey hunting folklore has always stressed the lonely gobbler at this time of year, it is almost always a sure bet that more than one of a spring group is a tom.

I can't count the times that I've seen spring flocks consisting of a half-dozen or so gobblers and a few hens. On one occasion, two days before the season opener on a cool, crisp morning with frost still on the grass and the sun rising over the end of a sere cornfield, I saw a magnificent backlit gobbler in full strut. The sunlight danced on his iridescent feathers and made a giant golden halo of his widely spread tail feathers. Gathered around him were 11 other turkeys, and I scanned every bird in that group with my binoculars. There were five hens and seven gobblers. Three of the gobblers had beards in the eight to 10-inch range.

The facts are plain and simple: Gobblers, except on rare occasions, travel in gangs. And they do this for good reason. A lone turkey, even a gobbler in his prime, is vulnerable. A solitary bird has only two eyes to detect a stalking fox, dog or coyote. Two or more turkeys can share the job of spotting predators. And when a predator attacks, the more birds that are present, the less the odds are that any one individual will be taken. Attacking predators often become confused when surrounded by potential meals. A half-dozen or so bodies clamoring skyward or racing through the brush is distracting. At such times, it is difficult to focus on a single bird. Think of the first time you flushed a covey of quail and you'll understand the problem that the predator has.

TO THE CASUAL OBSERVER, AGE AND SIZE SEEM TO DICTATE GOBBLER DOMINANCE.

With the approach of the spring mating urge, family groups, which have consisted of hens and the young of the year during the winter, drift toward traditional nesting areas. Mature gobblers, who have been traveling in much smaller bachelor flocks, start traveling with the family groups. Inevitably, the mature gobblers assert their dominance over the jakes and lesser toms. In response, the jakes group together on the flock's edge.

To the casual observer, age and size seem to dictate gobbler dominance. This is basically true. However, aggressive behavior has a decided effect, and many times, when a gang of gobblers comes in to the call, the bird having the longest beard and longest spurs and weighing the most is not the one that is strutting his stuff in front of the hen-folk.

A hunter from Pawlet, Vermont, sought a boss gobbler that had a large harem on a secluded farm in that state. The bird—a two-year-old 18-pounder with a seven-inch beard and three-quarters-inch spurs—fell to the hunter on the season's third day. The tom was neither big nor old by any standards. But there was evidence that it had been aggressive. It had several missing tail feathers, and its chest and underside were nearly nude—the result of fighting.

Two days after this bird fell, the farmer reported seeing a bigger gobbler with the harem. "It's the same gobbler that bossed the harem before the hunting season began," he said. "That other bird whipped him. Now he's back on top."

The second bird later fell to another hunter's gun. It weighed 21 pounds and had one-inch spurs and a 10-inch beard. It was probably a three- or four-year-old gobbler.

For most hunters, however, it's not important to know whether they are faced with a boss or a subordinate gobbler. What is important is for them to realize that there is usually more than one gobbler in any particular area.

How many gobblers can a hunter expect to find in an area? Usually, a newly hatched turkey clutch is half hens and half gobblers. Spring gobbler hunting reduces the gobbler-to-hen ratio, but even in heavily hunted areas, there are often five gobblers for every six to seven hens.

One May morning several years ago, I set up on a hardwood ridge in an area that I knew contained several gobblers. When I owl-hooted before dawn, a gobbler answered from his roost about 100 yards down the ridge to my left. I waited 10 minutes and then scratched out two soft hen yelps. The gobbler responded. I then went silent, and after listening to about 30 minutes of continuous gobbling off to my left, I heard several birds fly down in that area.

I was looking in the direction of the gobbling when I saw movement to my right. Two jakes had approached silently, and they now stood 20 yards away, staring at me. They made me out and scooted away. The gobbler to my left sounded off again. I clucked twice. He gobbled.

Again, I saw movement to my right. A third jake stared at me from the spot the first two had just vacated. He made me out and scooted away. I clucked again. The gobbler to my left answered. He was much closer this time.

I put the slate call away and slowly shouldered my shotgun. Two black bodies materialized 80 yards away to my left. The lead gobbler paused every few steps and turned around. The trailing gobbler, caught partly puffed up, would quickly deflate.

They were still out of range when I heard three quick shotgun blasts about 100 yards to my right. The gobblers froze. After five minutes of playing statue, they began moving toward me again. They were still 50 yards out when the second bird suddenly stretched its neck and shock-gobbled. Both birds then turned tails and raced back in the direction from which they had come.

A few seconds later, a towheaded hunter in partial camouflage walked up beside me. A jake with a two-inch beard dangled from his belt. "It's dangerous to use a gobble call in the woods," he said. He thought that the real gobble both of us had just heard was me using a gobble call! He then offered me a few gloating words of wisdom as he headed out to his car. "There ain't no sense hunting here now," he said. "I got the only gobbler in these woods."

In spite of knowing that more gobblers remained, I felt that my hunt was over. My visitor had shot one bird, then had walked right through the area where the two mature gobblers had fled to. Still, I stayed on and occasionally sent out a few yelps and clucks, but I did so without much enthusiasm.

An hour later, I admitted defeat. And as I stood to stretch my legs, a shock-gobble rattled the oak trees from 40 yards to my left. Then I was truly alone.

That one episode taught me a very valuable lesson. Now, when I see or hear a gobbler, I know that it's part of a gang, and I stay put even if someone else shoots near me.

Another hunt several years later further ingrained this lesson into my head. Ron Krause, a dark-haired, hard-hunting corrections officer from Massachusetts, stopped by my Vermont home one May afternoon to ask, "Can you tell me where to find a turkey?"

We spent the afternoon together, and at dusk, we roosted a gang of gobblers. We then moved a half-mile down the same road and roosted another gang under a stone escarpment on the same ridge.

We made plans. Because Ron is a better caller than me, we decided that he should hunt on his own. He was to move in on the second bunch of birds the next morning; I would move on the first group. But, as is par for the course with turkey hunting, several factors served to alter our plans.

It was very dark the next morning. Ron was unfamiliar with the hunting area, and his gobblers failed to respond to pre-dawn owl hooting. My gobblers, on the other hand, cooperated nicely.

Ron then innocently drifted toward my more vocal birds, and set up to my north, 300 yards from the gobblers. I set up in an abandoned pasture 80 yards east of the birds and on the other side of a 60-foot-wide marshy area. I had scouted these birds prior to the opener, and I knew that the boss gobbler, followed by his gang, usually sailed out across the marshy area to the pasture. Once there, he would typically strut and gobble in the area where my decoy now rested.

After a time, I decided to call, and a lusty gobble immediately answered from across the marsh. This time, however, instead of soaring across to my pasture, the group took a different route, staying on the ground on the other side of the wet area and moving north, toward Ron.

"I saw the beard," Ron told me later, "and knew that I was going to get my gobbler. He came right at me. Then I saw four more birds trailing behind him. The longbeard just kept gobbling.

"At the spring where the marsh starts, he turned south and started walking away from me. I called. He gobbled, but he wouldn't come back. About 100 yards separated us, and he was getting farther away with every step. Then I looked back and saw two birds running toward me. Both had small beards. I shot twice and had my limit." (Vermont's spring limit is two gobblers, and both may be taken the same day.)

Ron's two gobblers were jakes. But at the time, I had no idea who had shot or what had been taken.

The two shotgun blasts had silenced the area. I fumed. Somebody had stolen my gobbler. At that instant, I thought that it was the only one left in the woods.

The gray mood passed quickly, however, as I remembered that there were more gobblers. There always are. And because I hadn't heard the rest of the birds scatter at the shot, nor did I know whether or not they had seen whomever had done the shooting, I opted to stay put and let things calm down a bit. After about a five-minute wait, I clucked softly. A booming gobble sounded. The longbeard had evidently frozen at the shots, but he was now moving again. And he was headed my way.

Two boisterous slate-call clucks later, the strutting tom stepped into the pasture. That bird fell to patience and persistence.

THE LONGBEARD HAD EVIDENTLY FROZEN AT THE SHOTS, BUT HE WAS NOW MOVING AGAIN.

When Ron and I met later, we reconstructed the morning's hunt. We had taken three gobblers from a gang of five in less than 10 minutes and within 300 yards of each other—not bad for a "busted" hunt. It was obvious from the reactions of the birds that they had not been unduly alarmed by Ron's shots. They had no doubt heard a loud bang, but for turkeys and other woods dwellers, everyday life is filled with loud bangs. They hadn't as yet seen a predator, and they may have passed the noise off as a falling tree or a clap of thunder.

Sometimes, however, a flock of birds will scatter at the shot, even when they don't see the hunter. When this happens and the second hunter knows that the birds have dispersed without having been alarmed by a predator, the techniques used are a little different. The trick to get birds in under these circumstances is to begin calling again immediately. And don't be shy about your calling. Call loud and often. You are a lone hen, deserted by a bunch of "sissies" scared off by a falling tree. Let the gobblers know that they have nothing to fear. Occasionally, the entire harem will return. More often, a jake will sneak back to comfort that lonely hen pleading for male companionship.

Even spooked gobblers that first hear a hen and then see a hunter (such as the two mature toms that were scared off when the hunter with the jake approached me in the earlier story) rarely seem to associate the hen calls with the hunter. Gobblers will flee when they see a large, ominous figure approaching them in the woods, but they are probably still convinced that there is a hen in the area. They heard her. They also most likely believe that she saw the danger, too, and because of it, went silent. Once the danger passes, they expect to hear the hen call again.

The key in this situation is to give things time to calm down. Unfortunately, I had to learn this the hard way, because often in the past when I walked into a gobbler, I was usually as shocked as he was and instinctively tried calling him back. It never worked. This was probably because the gobbler was extremely wary after seeing a large figure walking through the woods. He might not have known exactly what frightened him, but he did know that whatever had spooked him certainly wasn't another turkey. Calling immediately after spooking a gobbler that has seen you often produces a "call-shy" bird.

EXPERIENCE HAS TAUGHT ME TO NEVER FOLLOW A SPOOKED GOBBLER.

Last spring, I situated myself in one of my favorite locations and began calling just as there was a hint of dawn in the eastern sky. Almost immediately, a gobbler responded from about 120 yards away. For an hour after first light, I called and that gobbler answered, but he would not come in. So I moved on him.

"I went about 200 yards to my right along a low ridge and began calling again. After two gobbling responses, a hen walked past me and toward the gobbler. A few minutes later, he went silent. A real hen had seduced my gobbler and taken him to places unknown.

I tried to follow, but 20 minutes later, with head hanging and feet plodding noisily along, I headed back toward my Jeep. My route took me through the area from where I had called earlier. I was just passing the tree that I'd set up against when another gobble startled me. I spun toward the sound, and saw a black body scurrying through the underbrush. I knew that I had been spotted.

Experience has taught me to never follow a spooked gobbler, as startled gobblers often run only 60 to 100 yards before stopping. Once stopped, they examine their backtrail to try to discover what startled them. If they see a hunter following, they'll leave the area.

Thus, after settling my shattered nerves, I slipped about 20 yards along my backtrail and set up. Thirty minutes later, after giving the tom ample time to calm down, I sent out a few soft clucks. Turkeys don't begin calling lustily after having seen a large predator in the area; they call softly and with some trepidation. Hunters should keep their calls soft and simple at such times; a cluck or two will do it.

After three series of clucks over a 15-minute period, I heard the gobbler coming back through the dry leaves. He never gobbled. He fell to a load of No. 6s a few minutes later.

I knew that this bird would come in silently. The area's gobbling boss bird had earlier gone off with the hen. Any gang member off chasing a hen on its own was obviously non-dominant. He had shock-gobbled when I had startled him, but that was simply a reflex action. Non-dominant birds do not gobble openly to hen calls.

The bottom line here is that a hunter should never give up on an area just because either a bird was spooked or another tom was taken in the vicinity. If the spooked bird saw the hunter clearly but was not pursued by him, the hunter is no more than a passing intrusion, and the bird can most times be called back after a time. If the bird was spooked by a shotgun blast, the second hunter should know that there are bound to be other gobblers around and that they, too, can be called in.

Wise hunters know that gobblers travel in gangs; they hear a nearby shot or listen to the story of another hunter's success, and thus know where they, too, can score on a spring turkey.

ON THE FINAL APPROACH

⟳◈⟲

by John Higley

CALLING IS IMPORTANT, BUT WOODSMANSHIP GETS YOU UP CLOSE AND PERSONAL WITH GOBBLERS.

"DAMN GREENHORN!" At one time or another, every turkey hunter I know has uttered those words—or much worse. And the loudest grumblers are often those who are novices themselves.

Terry Brumley and I aren't quite beginners, but we mumbled just the same last April when someone messed up our hunt. We were feeling plenty smug as we moved in on a gobbling northern California Rio Grande. But then came an owl hoot, a box call yelp, a crow call . . . and silence. Another hunter had heard the same gobbling we'd heard and, thanks to him, the turkey shut up for good. The other hunter probably never knew we were already set up on the bird. But no matter, our hunting for the morning was over.

Obviously, being a good caller is important to hunting turkeys. The problem with that other hunter we'd heard, though, wasn't bad calling; it was that he knew little about the right and wrong way to move in the woods, to locate birds and then to set up once a bird gobbles. Some hunters acquire the knack for this very quickly. For others it takes time to learn effective strategy in the turkey woods, whether on their own or at the side of an accommodating, experienced turkey hunter.

It's basic to remember that wild turkeys, inherently wary of everything that moves, rely mainly on keen eyesight as their first line of defense against predation. More than once, I've stepped carelessly into the open on one end of a grain field, meadow or ridgetop, only to see turkeys a quarter mile away start running for cover when they saw me. That's when I feel like hanging a "kick me" sign on my backside and begin muttering sharp words under my breath.

GOOD WOODSMANSHIP

The key is to see the turkey before the turkey sees you. To do this, experienced turkey hunters carefully utilize the contours of the terrain to hide their movements. By keeping a rise between you and the next field, taking advantage of a line of brush, standing in the shadows while you scan the openings for turkeys, or using binoculars to spot turkeys from afar, you can mask at least some of your normal movements. Stealth is obviously very important, so how and when you move depends largely on the type and amount of cover, and the terrain variations in your location.

"I hunt such a variety of terrain in the East and West," says Brad Harris of Lohman Game Calls, "that I have to adjust constantly during the season. Sometimes, out on the plains, I use a spotting scope to locate birds that might be out there a mile, then I figure out how to get into decent calling range. That sometimes means sneaking down creek washes, circling ridges or crawling on my hands and knees to take advantage of some little depression. You'd be surprised what you can get away with if you aren't afraid to get down and dirty."

Of course, your applied hunting skills should include more than stealth and eyesight. You will not be at your best as a turkey hunter until you learn how to really listen for the obvious—and not so obvious—sounds the birds make during their daily routine. When you call in an attempt to locate turkeys, by all means concentrate on hearing a reply from any direction. Don't chat with a friend, blow your nose or unwrap a candy bar. Take a deep breath and listen. Even when you're not calling, pay attention to the sounds you hear in the woods. You may hear a gobble at any time, but even if you don't you can sometimes detect other turkey sounds, such as a flock walking through leaves, scratching, flying and even the drumming sounds a gobbler makes when he struts.

If you are uncertain where the neighborhood toms are at the moment, call a little before hiking to the crest of a ridge or exposing yourself to open ground. Before calling at all, look around and find a place to set up quickly in case a gobbler responds from close range. Always try to locate a spot to sit where your vision won't be hindered by tall weeds or other obstructions and where no sticks or branches will make a long wait uncomfortable. Remember, too, to take a second glance around for poison ivy, poison oak, snakes, ants or yellow jackets.

One time, easing down a ridge during an afternoon hunt, I spotted a trio of Wyoming toms before they saw me. The ridge was sloping, and every few feet I stopped to gaze ahead at new ground, much like a house cat stalking a mouse. It was during one such pause that my eyes focused on an odd shape looming above a fold of land—a shape that immediately started the adrenaline flowing. It was the top few inches of a Merriam's turkey's fanned tail, no more than 40 yards away. Quickly, I backed up and crouched next to a nearby pine tree. I regained my composure somewhat and yelped a couple of times with a diaphragm, whereby not one but three toms strutted into view. The one I killed weighed 19½ pounds and wore a 9½-inch beard, which is very respectable for a Merriam's gobbler.

I LIKE TO BETTER MY ODDS BY TAKING A FEW STEPS, THEN PAUSING LIKE A REAL TURKEY DOES.

THE LAST MOVE

As any experienced turkey hunter will tell you, moving in on a tom is sometimes as necessary as covering lots of ground searching for him in the first place. But by the same token, moving into a good calling position is not the same as stalking into shotgun range—which can be dangerous if there are other hunters in the vicinity. Obviously, anytime you move, it's important to be cautious and to put safety first. For your own sake, be sure to unload your shotgun chamber, especially in rough terrain. There will be time to reload when you reach a spot from which to call.

But what does the experienced turkey hunter do if the toms aren't being especially vocal on a particular day or the hens are leading them to parts unknown? One strategy for locating toms and following their progress is to use a shock call of some sort. The most popular shock calls duplicate the sounds of crows and barred owls. And some hunters, especially out West, rely on elk bugles and predator calls, as well.

HUNTING TECHNIQUES

USING TERRAIN

Superior eyesight is a turkey's first line of defense. When moving into a set-up position or when trying to locate birds, always use the terrain to your advantage. Never call from the crest of a rise; call just below it.

CONCEALED CALLING

When possible, use available cover and good camouflage to shield you from a turkey's view. For example, never step into an open field. Linger in the shadows of field-edge brush before calling, but don't box yourself in—be safe!

ON THE MOVE

Before pausing to call in an opening like this, it's critical to first locate an area to set up, just in case you get an instant reply from an unseen gobbler. This hunter will be caught dead-to-rights if a gobbler responds to his yelps.

LISTEN UP

No, this hunter isn't playing charades. He's listening intently for turkey sounds—not only gobbles and yelps. Cupping your ears will help amplify hard-to-hear turkey noises, such as scratching in the leaves or clucking.

SEEING'S BELIEVING

Never hunt turkeys without bringing along a pair of binoculars. Whether hunting farm fields or ridgetops, spotting birds before they see you will give you a decided advantage. Use binoculars often, especially during midday hunts.

BOTTOMS UP

Green, lush bottoms are great places to find gobblers in the spring. Here, gobblers can be noticed by hens that may find good nesting cover nearby. This hunter needs to move cautiously, however, to avoid spooking birds in this open terrain.

SUCCESS

Woodsmanship and good calling make a successful combination for spring gobblers. Know how and when to move through the woods, as well as how and when to call, and you'll be lugging out longbeards with regularity.

The basic idea, no matter where you are, is to elicit a reflex gobble. Then, having located your tom, you can move into position and try to call him in.

But what about the human noise factor? The idea that a turkey hunter can creep through the woods like a cloud of smoke is a pipe dream. Not even snakes are entirely silent, and every animal, from squirrels to deer to cows, makes noise.

"Noise alone doesn't affect turkeys much, unless they catch movement, too," explains expert turkey hunter Ray Eye. "But when it's dry, I like to better my odds by taking a few steps, then pausing like a real turkey does, and maybe scratching in the leaves a little. I usually make a few hen calls now and then to add to the realism. And I'm very careful not to break branches, clear my throat or talk out loud when I'm with another hunter." You'll know you've arrived as a turkey hunter when you start seeing, hearing and calling gobblers that formerly would have seen, heard and fled from you first. Hunting wild turkeys, of course, is never a sure thing, anyway. But your effectiveness depends on much more than just making turkey noises. The challenge is to learn and practice a wide variety of other hunting skills—stealth, using cover and woodsmanship—at the same time. Remember, good calling is important, but good woodsmanship is vital.

⇒◆⇐

TOMS TAKE TIME

by Kathy Etling

PATIENCE IS A VIRTUE—AND ONE THAT HUNTERS NEED LOTS OF WHEN THEIR FIRST CALLS DON'T BRING THAT GOBBLER HIGH-STEPPING IN.

AS I CREPT INTO THE PINE GROVE well before dawn, I already knew that the spot held gobblers. I'd roosted the birds the evening before, so I was sure that two, maybe three toms were now perched within 100 yards of my setup. I waited, savoring the possibilities, knowing full well that when you're after wild turkeys, possibilities are often the only thing left to hold on to at the end of the day.

When the first gobble echoed through the woods, I gripped my shotgun tighter. Just maybe this would be the kind of hunt that all those guys on the videos seem to have—the kind where gobblers almost run hunters over in their eagerness to get to the calling.

Usually, though, I work hard for my turkeys, and as the minutes passed it looked like this hunt would be no different. The several turkeys that ended up sounding off obstinately refused to come in, no matter how often I called or which calls I used.

Finally, a hen moseyed past, heading toward the reluctant gobblers, and as soon as the toms saw her, their reluctance disappeared. They flew off the roost and started gobbling with gusto. But even though they were now on the ground, it didn't help me a bit: From where I was sitting I still couldn't see them.

I waited in suspense for more than three hours. The first hour was exciting, as gobbles rang out every couple of minutes, often in response to my calls. So I knew that the toms knew where I was. I hoped that once the boss gobbler tired of that particular hen, he'd be back for the one that wouldn't come in: me!

But after three hours I wasn't so sure. Oh, I'd hear a gobble every now and then, but when I did it would sound almost indifferent. I stayed where I was because I'd been in the same predicament many times before, yet often had come home with a gobbler, anyway. I wasn't about to give up.

My patience paid off halfway through the fourth hour. I hadn't heard a peep for about 20 minutes, and then just one gobble rang out—from a completely different direction from those I'd been hearing all morning. I eased my shotgun toward the sound just as a tom darted into view, and when the bird moved behind a cedar, I brought the gun to my shoulder. When the gobbler stepped out, I fired. I jumped up to claim my prize and discovered that he was a tom worth waiting for—23½ pounds, with a 10-inch beard and 1¼-inch spurs. A real trophy.

I was lucky in a way. When I first learned to hunt turkeys, patience wasn't an option, it was a rule. My husband and I decided to try turkey hunting back in the mid-1960s, when the sport was still a novelty across much of the United States. At that time we hadn't yet bought our own hunting ground, so we were fortunate to find a 400-acre farm to hunt just an hour from our home. We soon discovered that the farmer had very definite ideas about turkey hunting and safety and I'm glad he did.

The farmer allowed each hunter just 40 or so acres on which to hunt. Each had to stay on his own parcel of land until he either killed a bird or decided to come back to the house. Forty acres isn't a very big chunk of real estate, especially when you're turkey hunting. But I soon learned that it was big enough, if I had enough patience.

At first, with no one to teach me the basics, I was lost in this newfangled sport. Even so, by staying in one spot and making just three yelps on my box call every 20 minutes, I called in a gobbler that very first year. It didn't matter much that he saw me and ran off before I could shoot. I'd learned a valuable lesson: Turkeys often will come sneaking in after just one or two gobbles.

A DOUBLE DOSE OF PATIENCE IS PRESCRIBED WHEN YOU'RE AFTER ONE OF THESE CALL-SHY BIRDS.

By the time I killed my first gobbler I could sit for hours in one spot. And once I'd bagged my first bird, I began killing turkeys regularly. Patience, I knew, worked. But when we finally bought our own land, I gave in to temptation and ran hog-wild. It was wonderful having the freedom to chase birds anywhere. But when I did, my success rate plummeted. My calling hadn't changed, but my patience had. I soon realized that I'd succeeded previously mainly because of my ability to wait.

Most of us live life in the fast lane. One of the pitfalls of this lifestyle is expecting results . . . now! Many of today's hunting videos contribute to this instant-success mentality. They make turkey hunting look like a snap, but don't inform their unsuspecting viewers that unless you're either an outstanding caller, or hunting an area with little competition, turkey hunting can be anything but easy. The key to killing turkeys no matter where you hunt is patience. It's a key that a number of well-known turkey hunters use to consistently bag birds. Experts like Joe Drake of Columbus, Georgia, and Mark Drury of Bloomsdale, Missouri, know the virtues of sitting tight.

I hunted with Drake last year in Georgia. Of all the "pros" I've hunted with, his tactics more closely resemble my own than anyone else's. "I learned the hard way," Drake confessed. "Moving too soon and bumping a bird that's coming in slowly or silently is a common mistake among turkey hunters, even among those who should know better. At times I've moved when I thought bird wasn't coming in, then called again only to hear the gobbler answer from where I just was. It's frustrating to sit and wait, but I've found that patience is one of the most important factors in becoming a successful turkey hunter."

Drake's not only a top turkey hunter, but he's also a world-class caller. In 1990 he lost the Grand National turkey calling contest by just one point. That same year he won the friction call division of the Dixie Classic. Nevertheless, Drake rates patience higher than calling ability for consistent turkey hunting success.

"When a bird gobbles several times in response to your call," Drake explained, "he already knows where you are, so it's time to shut up. Over-calling is a big problem today. Most every hunter in the woods likes to hear himself call, so the birds quickly get call-shy. Hunters who go out early to 'practice' calling turkeys aren't doing anyone a favor. It just makes the birds warier and harder to call in."

A double dose of patience is prescribed when you're after one of these call-shy birds, according to Drake. "Turkey hunting has changed drastically in the last couple of years," he said. "There are many more hunters in the woods, and all of them are calling—a lot! People say that today's turkeys don't gobble as much, and I believe that's true. Gobblers have been fooled before, either before or during the season, so why should they run right in?"

Drake has bagged many birds that other hunters have felt were too cagey to kill. Like the bird that was holed up in a burn on some heavily hunted public ground. "One hunter had been working this stubborn old gobbler ever since opening day," Drake recalled. "A couple of times I tried calling him, too, but didn't even get a response. One day I went by the burn again and did some cutting just to see if the tom would answer. Hens 'cut' to demand a gobbler's attention. It's a loud, long, insistent call. Anyway, it was late in the morning, and I was surprised when the bird gobbled back. So I eased on into the burn, found a spot to set up, and yelped softly three times. The bird gobbled again from the same spot. I didn't call again for 40 minutes. All that time, he didn't gobble.

"When I did call again, that tom gobbled right behind me. He'd completely circled me and was so close I could actually hear him running. I turned slowly so I could see him. It was sort of funny when I finally did spot him. With each step, his foot would kick up a puff of soot from the burn. He walked behind a tree, and when he stepped out I killed him."

Drake feels that patience has its place in calling, too. "Each time you call," he said, "you run the risk of stopping a gobbler and making him strut. This is called 'hang-up time' because birds won't always gobble when they're strutting. Hunters who don't hear constant gobbling may think the bird they were calling has lost interest. But that's not always true. I've had gobblers come in just spitting and drumming, making that almost inaudible sound that means they're puffed out and strutting. If you can hear that sound, the bird is already within shotgun range."

I FEEL THAT BEING PATIENT IS AS IMPORTANT AS KNOWING THE LAND YOU'RE HUNTING.

Waiting up to 1½ hours for a bird is common, according to Drake. He's sat as long as three hours waiting for a turkey to show. That's remarkable when you consider that many top callers will readily leave a gobbling bird if they don't feel that he's "hot" enough.

Mark Drury is another champion caller who feels that many gobblers are worth the wait. Drury is only 24 years old, but his turkey hunting experience would fill a couple of books. Growing up in prime turkey territory, Drury was an avid hunter by the time he was 14. He read everything he could on the subject and now he is one of the top callers in the nation. He is a two-time holder of the Natural Voice World Calling Championships, but he admitted, "Sometimes the best call is no call at all."

A gobbler that answers early then shuts up might sneak in later for a midmorning rendezvous.

Drury is known for persistence. His first longbeard taught him the value of patience. "I'd been playing 'cat and mouse' with this gobbler for a couple of hours," he explained. "I'd move too soon and he'd be where I'd just moved from. Finally, I sat down and waited him out. It took an hour before he finally appeared, but when he did, he was mine."

Patience came in handy this past season, as well. Drury and his brother, Terry, stayed after one gobbler for eight days before Terry finally killed the big 25½-pound turkey.

"I feel that being patient is as important as knowing the land you're hunting," Drury stated. "Those two factors together account for 75 percent of what it takes to succeed as a turkey hunter. Knowing turkeys' habits is worth another 15 percent. I really believe that calling only counts for 5 or 10 percent.

"I know that I can call, but I kill most of my turkeys by outmaneuvering, outsmarting or out-waiting them."

Out-waiting a gobbler came in handy when Drury was hunting a Mississippi hardwood bottom two years ago. "I'd been after this really tough turkey," he explained. "On the third afternoon, I asked my friend Randy Panek if he'd like to come with me.

"We got into the area where I knew the gobbler had been and I yelped with my voice. He didn't answer, so I yelped again. This time, the bird gobbled. When Randy and I got closer, we could tell that the bird wasn't alone. He was with a whole group of turkeys on the other side of a cane thicket."

THE OLD BIRD RESPONDED IMMEDIATELY, AND AFTER HOURS OF STALLING, CAME CHARGING IN.

A big canebrake is a formidable obstacle that can stop a hunter flat in his tracks. And that's exactly what this one did. Because Drury and Panek could hear the bird gobbling on the other side of the brake, they sat down where they were to call. "Our calling really got the flock fired up," Drury said. "Hens started calling, and then the jakes began gobbling. Whenever the jakes gobbled, the boss would gobble, too. We went on for two hours like that before we decided to shut up.

"When we got quiet, so did the turkeys. We were afraid they would leave, so we began to call again. The turkeys got fired up all over again, then everything began to die down. We could tell the flock was beginning to lose interest. We could also hear them starting to move away."

This Mississippi hardwood bottom was big and open with lots of huge trees. A few cane thickets provided cover, but the two hunters knew that if they tried to move around the cane, the turkeys would see them. They had to keep sitting tight like they had for the past three hours. As roosting time approached, Drury realized that this was when the boss would be most vulnerable. He decided to use a "jealousy" tactic and made a couple of jake yelps. That did the trick. The old bird responded immediately, and after hours of stalling, came charging in. Within 30 seconds the cane parted and the hunters could see the gobbler. Panek killed the bird when he was just 15 yards away.

The bottom line in all this is that good things come to those who sit tight. If you finally want to get the upper hand on spring gobblers, try using a dose of patience. It's a key to turkey hunting success that is often underutilized, but one worth its "wait" in toms. You may never run and gun again.

⟵⬦⟶

TACKLE A TOM

by Michael Pearce

BOWHUNTING TURKEYS ALLOWS NO ROOM FOR ERROR. THESE TIPS WILL HELP YOU PREPARE.

FEW WHO HAVE TRIED spring turkey hunting will deny that it is one of the most exciting prospects in American hunting. This same group of turkey hunting fanatics will also quickly say that it's the calling that makes the springtime sport so special.

The excitement of a turkey hunt seems to build like a Stephen King thriller as a hard-gobbling tom is lured to the hunter's hen calls. A dialogue of hunter's yelps and turkey's gobbles climax as the tom comes into sight, perhaps nervous, or maybe displaying for what he thinks is a prospective mate. Actually taking the bird with a pizza-size pattern of shotgun pellets can seem anticlimactic compared with the excitement of the calling. For that reason, more and more sportsmen are prolonging the challenge and excitement of turkey season by trying to take a spring gobbler with a bow and arrow.

The switch from gun to bow presents a new set of challenges for the turkey hunter, not the least of which is simply getting ready for a shot. Decoys, blinds, calling and timing will help, but drawing a bow without being seen or heard by a wild turkey is one of hunting's greatest tests of stealth.

"Just getting drawn on them without being seen is the toughest part," says Jim Holdenried, a well-known Missouri bowhunter with more than two decades of spring turkey experience. "If there is any way they can see the movement, they will. They are paying attention and looking for something when they come to calls. Turkeys are always alert and looking."

Even with the hardest part past them, bowhunters who come to full draw face challenges. Number one is knowing where to arrow the bird. Recent talk has surfaced about taking head shots with blunts or Zwickey "Judo" points. (Be sure to check state regulations before trying.) Some hunters claim that the non-penetrating heads bring a clean kill when they strike the head or neck, but merely injure a bird if it strikes any other part of the body. Most experienced turkey bowhunters refrain from trying a head shot. For one reason, the target is small; a turkey's head is about the size of a 50-cent piece. And hunters who have spent much time in the woods with wild turkeys know that the birds seldom strike statuelike poses. Instead, their necks are continuously twisting, and their heads are bobbing, even when their feet are planted firmly in place.

Like most big-game bowhunters, the majority of America's turkey bowhunters prefer to put a sharp broadhead into the birds' heart-and-lung region. It's a small area, roughly the size of an orange, so pinpoint accuracy is critical. So is knowing where to find the tom's vitals.

"A lot of people really don't know where the chest cavity is on a bird," said Toby Bridges, an experienced turkey bowhunter. "From the time we begin practicing for hunts, we are taught to aim low in the chest on big game animals. But if you shoot there on a turkey, all you're going to hit is white meat."

SHOT PLACEMENT

A turkey's heart and lung area is high in the chest cavity. Here are the best aim points depending on the turkey's position:

A

B

C

(A) High in the back—offers the spine as well as the kill zone; (B and C) For broadside birds, aim for wing butt; (D) A bowhunter's best opportunity—aim at the base of the fan. (E) A poor time to shoot—pick an area between the neck and beard for a kill zone that lies between the bird's wings.

D

E

Experienced bowhunters like Bridges admit that it takes a little practice to quickly recognize the target area of a turkey. The target area on a wild turkey sits high on its body, just below the spine, basically between the wings.

The target area seems to change, however, when a tom breaks into strut.

"A strutting turkey changes the whole thing," Bridges said. "You shoot high on them and all you're going to hit is feathers. It takes a little extra studying to realize where to make a good side shot, and even [where to aim] a frontal shot because of the birds' puffed feathers and body structure."

Many bowhunters prefer a going-away shot on a strutting gobbler. For one thing, the fanned tail blocks the head, providing an excellent chance to draw and aim. The turkey also provides a precise target. The aiming point is directly at the base of the fan (at the anus).

Over the last few years, bow-and-arrow turkey hunting has become popular enough for manufacturers to offer some specialized equipment. Most avid turkey bowhunters say any well-tuned hunting bow will work well for springtime hunts. Many bowhunters simply use their favorite deer-hunting bow, usually set at a lower poundage.

"It never hurts most deer hunters to back their bow down a bit if they're going turkey hunting," Bridges said. "As long as they can still shoot it accurately, it's not a bad idea for bowhunters to crank their bows down past what they may shoot on deer.

"You never really know how long you're going to have to stay at full draw on turkeys," he added. "Sometimes it's a few seconds, sometimes it's an honest few minutes. Even with the high let-off rates of some bows, there's a big difference between holding a bow set at 80 pounds and a bow set at 60 pounds. Besides, there's no reason you can't kill a turkey with a 50 or maybe even a 45-pound-pull bow. In fact, some hunters suggest it's best to use a lower poundage bow to prevent arrows from totally passing through a turkey."

Some hunters believe that if the arrow stays in the bird, the turkey will be hampered in its escape and more easily recovered (because they don't leave much of a blood trail). This is especially true with a broadside shot placed at the wing vent. The broadhead will enter the bird's chest cavity, and the arrow's shaft will hamper the turkey's wing beats.

Currently there are several broadheads on the market, including the Wasp Turkey Spur and the Muzzy Turkey Thumper, designed to reduce penetration while increasing shock on impact. Some companies also offer products that fit between the broadhead and the arrow to stop pass-through shots. It's worth mentioning that there are a number of experienced hunters who say they prefer their arrow to do the maximum amount of damage even if it means passing through the bird. These hunters attach the same broadhead they use for deer hunting.

Another popular, but somewhat contested, tool for bowhunting turkeys is a string tracker. Similar to a bowfishing reel, a string tracker's spool of white or brightly colored string is attached to the bow and connected to the arrow. When a turkey is hit but doesn't go down immediately, the string spools out with the bird, and in theory makes recovery much easier. The hunter can simply follow the string to the bird.

Some hunters, including Lyle Prell, a highly respected turkey bowhunter, place complete confidence in string trackers. Others, like Holdenried and Bridges, have their reservations, saying that the string could snag on brush or affect accuracy. They also argue that inexperienced hunters could see string trackers as a shortcut to accurate arrow placement.

But there are no shortcuts in this, or any other type of bowhunting. There is simply no substitute for good woodsmanship, knowledge of the species, and the ability to consistently put a razor-sharp broadhead into the turkey's vital zone. Those who possess these three key ingredients and a little luck will have an excellent chance of reaching the pinnacle of America's fastest-growing, and most addictive, hunting sport.

BOWBAG A GOBBLER

by Jim Churchill

CALLING A GOBBLER INTO GUN RANGE
IS HARD ENOUGH, BUT IF YOU'RE LOOKING FOR
AN EVEN GREATER CHALLENGE,
TRY HUNTING HIM WITH BOW AND ARROW.

"GOBBLE, GOBBLE, GOBBLE," rolled across the pine and maple-covered ridges, as a turkey gobbler served notice to any lonesome hens within hearing that he was ready and willing. I grinned and elbowed the figure standing next to me in the feeble light. "Sounds like a live one," I told my son-in-law, Dennis Pohl.

I slipped the Penns Woods diaphragm call into my mouth and blew my best rendition of a young hen turkey in search of a mate. Before the last note fell from the call, the gobbler called back.

We crept slowly along in the direction of the last noise, putting each foot down carefully. Then, we stopped and set up, and I called again. The gobbler's answer was so loud that we almost jumped.

"Can't be more than 30 yards away," Dennis whispered. "Let me get in front; might get a chance for a shot." We inched forward some more, and Dennis suddenly gripped my arm. "There he is," he mouthed.

The gobbler was a magnificent sight. His pale blue head gleamed in the pink light, and a virile beard projected from his chest. White wing tips accented the gleaming black feathers covering most of his husky body. Every inch of that bird projected confidence and masculinity. As we watched, his neck jerked forward and another gobble boomed through the woods.

Dennis carefully and slowly drew his bow, held, then released. His arrow shot forward—missing the bird's back by the width of a knife blade. The bird squatted quickly when the arrow passed over his back and was out of sight in a few seconds.

We chuckled to each other, the tension of the past few minutes washed away by the escaping bird. "Well, you have to say this," Dennis exclaimed, "we got within shooting distance of that bird. Just my bad shooting kept us from getting him."

But I didn't hold him responsible. Even a good bow shot such as Dennis might have trouble connecting on a wild turkey.

Encouraged by the events of the past few minutes, we continued to shift calling positions, trying to get another gobbler to answer. When we didn't, we went back to the truck. A short ride and another long walk brought us to a wooded hillside overlooking a field that had grown up to weeds and tall grass. Clover, young rye grass, and some winter-ravaged oats offered the turkeys succulent dining opportunities.

We believe wholeheartedly in pre-season scouting, and Dennis had located this field weeks before the season opened. On his way to work in the morning, he'd stop by to check for birds. He took along a notebook, and whenever he saw turkeys he'd jot down the time, temperature, wind direction and weather. He also paid particular attention to the location of the turkeys in the field. Armed with this information, we could predict when the turkeys would come out, and about where they would be in the field at a specific time.

By watching this and other fields, we noticed that turkeys are most likely to feed early when a cold night is followed by a warm day. This turned out to be especially true when there was little or no wind. Turkeys seem to dislike wind and will stay out of fields if they can't find a part of the opening that is protected. On warm, still-rainy mornings, they sleep a little later but will almost certainly feed and stay in the open for a long time. This type of morning is almost ideal for bowhunting because the hunter can move quietly and get into position before the turkeys come to feed.

A problem that the bowhunter must overcome, even when ambushing turkeys, is the turkey's sharp vision and superb reactions. When wild turkeys see a suspicious movement, they won't wait to find out what caused it. They'll lower their heads and start running. Sometimes, they'll even take off flying, like a grouse. Usually, the bowhunter won't have nearly enough time to shoot.

We have developed a method to forewarn the bowhunter of the arrival of turkeys in a field—even when they come by way of deep grass where they can't be easily seen. We stretch monofilament fishing line across the trail about four inches above the ground. One end is secured to a sturdy anchor, such as a tree trunk, and the other is tied to a weed or shrub.

The first turkey that walks the trail will stretch the fishing line, causing the weed or shrub to wiggle. Interestingly, the birds will not spook, thinking instead that it is merely another natural woods obstacle. Then, we know that the flock is coming, and we should either draw or get ready to draw. Compound bows provide an advantage because they can be drawn and held for a longer time than longbows or recurves. Arrows tipped with wide broadheads are preferred.

In one corner of the field, we built a blind of dead sticks covered with dead grass and weeds. The blind was located about 20 feet from the trail that the turkeys often used when coming into the field.

When we reached the field, Dennis sneaked into the blind while I sat about 100 feet away, hidden under the spreading branches of a balsam tree.

I did this so that when I called, the birds would home in on me instead of the shooter. We have noticed that a wild turkey has an uncanny ability to pinpoint a sound. He doesn't just have a general idea of where the sound came from; he knows exactly where it originated. But if the turkeys were looking at me, this would give Dennis a chance to draw and shoot without being seen. By hunting in pairs, with one doing the calling and the other the shooting, we can sometimes get the turkeys to come within 20 feet of the shooter without their discovering him—ideal bow range.

We waited until 10 a.m. for the birds to show up, and when they didn't, we decided that they had already fed and left by the time we arrived. But because they might still be resting nearby, I decided to call in an attempt to bring them in before the noon quitting hour.

I called at 10-minute intervals, giving the assembly call with a dose of what I refer to as the "gobbler threat" call. The threat call is given by the dominant bird, or "boss gobbler," and it serves to warn other gobblers that they are on his territory.

It worked too well. The third rendition of the call brought a response from an angry gobbler deep in the woods. He called again in less than a minute, much closer, and when I answered, the gobbler ran right up to me, bobbing his head. He seemed to have fire in his eyes. It happened so fast that I didn't have time to signal Dennis, who was turning his head from side to side, excitedly trying to locate the bird that he knew was nearby.

When the gobbler was within 10 feet of me, he skidded to a stop, recognized the possibility of danger and quickly changed from a combatant to a fugitive. I actually felt the air current from his beating wings and ducked from the booming sound of this departure.

The next morning, we decided to work our way near the roost tree in the area where we had missed the first gobbler. Turkeys are shrewd birds, but they do stay in a relatively small territory and roost in the same area, often in the same tree. Therefore, we reasoned that we might get another chance if we could get close to the roost tree.

When it got light enough to see, gobblers started calling on either side of us, but "our" bird was silent.

"I think I can wake him up," I whispered.

I blew on my owl hooter call. No answer. I blew again. Silence. I waited five minutes and called again. He never made a sound, and we began to wonder whether he was close by. I tried the crow call. Sometimes, a gobbler will answer a crow call when he won't sound off for the barred owl's notes.

Suddenly, a long series of turkey clucks and the sound of wings penetrated the silence.

"The fly-down call," I reminded Dennis. "Our bird just flew down to the ground. He can't be more than 50 yards away."

We found cover, and I started calling, using the "lonesome-hen" call. The gobbler answered immediately, but the sound was halfhearted and faint, seemingly more ritualistic than genuine. When he called the second time, he was farther away.

Some gobblers seem to recognize a certain call. If they have been spooked by a shot or the sight of a human after being called in, they won't respond very readily again. Apparently, our gobbler remembered that call. Changing tones sometimes helps. Therefore, I carry several diaphragm calls with me and keep trying different calls until the gobbler finds one to his liking.

MOST GOBBLERS
WILL NOT ROOST WITH HENS.

To get this bird, however, we would have to change our calling location. We eased our way along a woods road, careful to avoid snapping twigs or rustling the dried leaves. Suddenly, Dennis held up his hand. About 50 yards ahead, I could see a gobbler and about five or six hens feeding in a patch of clover on the road.

We crept into a clump of aspen on the side of the road. I decided to try to call the birds by using the young-bird assembly, or kee-kee run, call. This high-pitched series of five notes is usually used for calling turkeys in the fall, but I hoped that it would attract the young hens. Then, the gobbler might follow them into shooting range.

One hen broke off from the group when I called and walked swiftly toward us. In a few seconds, she was only 10 yards away. Then, she froze, eyes fixed on us, trying to decide whether we were dangerous. For a full minute, she watched us without moving. She then pecked the ground a few times, walked closer and, without haste, angled off to one side and disappeared into the underbrush.

I shifted my weight, but the faint rustling sound gave us away, confirming her suspicions. She gave a quick series of alarm putts,

and all of the turkeys walked briskly into the thick cover. Our chances for a shot disappeared for the day.

That afternoon, I remembered a strategy that expert turkey hunter Kenneth Waterworth had described when my son and I hunted with him in the Mark Twain National Forest near Lebanon, Missouri.

"Most gobblers will not roost with hens," he said. "Usually, the hens are setting on their nests, or for some other reason will have separated from the gobblers by the afternoon. A gobbler goes to roost early enough so that he can gobble a few times, telling the hens where he is. He hopes that they will go to him early the next morning. He reminds them by gobbling again when he wakes up.

"The hunter can go in the late afternoon, listen for the gobbler to go to roost and then get between him and his hens early the next morning. Rested and energetic in the morning, he will usually come to the call."

In the afternoon, we climbed a ridge overlooking the cutover area where the gobbler often roosted. Just as the sun disappeared for the day, a faint gobble reached us. I focused my 7X50 binoculars on the few standing trees and spotted the bird as he flew from the ground into a tall basswood tree. The leaves were not fully formed on the tree, and I could see him as he sidestepped along the limb until he reached the trunk.

We scrambled as fast as we could to get close to the gobbler. When we were about 100 yards away, I called to the gobbler with all of the volume I could muster from my diaphragm call. The gobbler answered. That was exactly what we were looking for. Often, a gobbler will remember a lonesome hen call that he hears just before dark. Perhaps he dreams about it. If he hears the same call at daybreak, he usually will come to the call.

The strategy worked perfectly the next morning—except for one thing. After the turkey flew down from the roost, he started toward us and "hung up" about 40 yards away. There, in plain sight, he strutted back and forth in a little clearing. Well within range for a heavy-gauge shotgun, but much too far for a bowshot.

I motioned to Dennis, and we walked directly away from the gobbler, careful to stay behind a stand of evergreens so that he couldn't see us. Some gobblers are confused and intrigued by a "hen" that walks away from them. They follow and sometimes walk right up to the caller. But he again stopped about 40 yards away and gobbled. We moved again, but he lost interest.

We spent the next two days hunting other areas, returning each afternoon to watch for the gobbler to return to his customary perch. Finally, on the third evening we located the gobbler in his roost. This time, we decided to try a different strategy. The next morning, Dennis set up near the little clearing where the turkey had stopped before. I walked about 25 yards away to call. If the turkey strutted again in the clearing, he would provide a good shot, even for a bowhunter.

Daylight finally came, and a lusty gobble rolled across the silent forest. To my mind, a turkey gobble is one of the most thrilling sounds in nature. It courses down my spine like the whistle of a bull elk or a timber wolf's howl.

That gobbler must have flown down immediately after the note from my call reached him. He had about 100 yards to travel to reach the clearing, but Dennis saw him less than two minutes after hearing him fly down. The turkey strode majestically into the tiny opening and started strutting for the hen with the sweet voice, his head glowing blood-red.

Dennis drew, waited for the target to turn sideways and released. The bird moved and walked right out of the trajectory of the arrow. It streaked over the turkey's head, clattered across the clearing and drove into a dirt hump. The turkey jumped, stopped strutting and fixed his keen eyes on the exact spot where the string noise had originated.

Dennis tried to remove another arrow from the bow quiver for a second shot. But the slight sound the arrow made when it snapped loose from its mount gave him away. The bird was running at full speed in a split second and was out of sight before Dennis could draw and shoot.

"From now on, I'm going to have a spare arrow ready to shoot," Dennis told me later. "I believe that I would have had a second shot if I had." The gobbler had escaped again, but he was using up his chances.

Hours of legwork and listening to the sounds of gobbling as the bird went about his daily activities helped us locate a stand of oak trees that still had a considerable quantity of acorns lying on the ground under the trees. Acorns are prime turkey feed, and even when they have lain under the snow all winter, the birds will eagerly seek them out.

The gobbler often visited this location during midmorning after his harem of hens had gone to nest. Gobblers don't eat much when they are in full "rut," but they do go to feeding locations—probably to look for hens.

The oak patch was located at the edge of a pine plantation, and we used the thick trees as a ready-made blind. I set up to call behind a log at the opposite edge of the oak stand to distract the gobbler when he came into the stand. To make sure that Dennis would be ready to shoot when the turkey arrived, we strung monofilament fishing line across several trails.

We were in place before daylight, but except for one lone hen that apparently had a nest nearby, no turkeys arrived until about 9:30. Then, as though to warn us, the gobbler sounded off a few hundred yards away. After what seemed like an hour, a bough jerked and the monarch stepped cautiously out of the pines. I shook the gobbler call. This seemed to infuriate the bird. He fanned his feathers and began a war dance. Closer and closer he came.

Then, feathers flew as the arrow found its mark, and the turkey flopped onto his side. He quickly got to his feet, ran a few steps and dropped again. Dennis sprinted from the blind and pounced on the bird. He was finally ours.

⇒◆⇐

THE LONGEST YARDS

---

by Michael Hanback

SOME TURKEY HUNTING SCENARIOS ARE SO CONFOUNDING, THE GOBBLERS MAY AS WELL BE MILES AWAY.

A VIRGINIA MOUNTAIN TURKEY once treated me and my brother-in-law to a magnificent solo of roost gobbling. Then, when the bird pitched from his tree, he wouldn't commit an inch to our yelps and purrs, even though there wasn't a real hen for miles. In fact, this guy was so sure of scoring elsewhere he *ran* from our overtures. It's that kind of arrogance that can really get to you.

"Let's dog that bird," I said to Brian. He was game, and we took off.

We followed our ridge-running tom for more than an hour, crow calling to keep a line on him. We moved fast, sweating up hillsides and gliding down hollows, keeping our distance and hiding in foliage so the bird couldn't make us.

The last time that tom hammered our crow calls, he was cresting a sunlit knoll, a perfect strutting ground. I switched to a raspy diaphragm and threw out a sharp series of cutts. *Gaaaarrrraaoobble!* I cutt again, just to make sure, and the tom roared back from the same spot.

We stopped him! Actually, the bird had stopped on his own, but it had to be in an area where he felt comfortable calling in the "hen." We obliged by circling around and setting up above the knoll. I yelped once, the tom broke our way and Brian nailed him with a charge of No. 6s.

We call that "bird-dogging," the first of eight deadly calling techniques outlined below that should help you make some sense out of the most confounding turkey hunting situations.

Try bird-dogging finicky gobblers that shun your calls and steadily walk away. Use a loud, high-pitched crow call (or hawk whistle or pileated woodpecker call) to monitor the bird—he's got to gobble frequently and reveal his travel path for this tactic to work. If the bird finally stops to strut, sneak as close as you dare and set up above him. Then switch over to hen calling and reel him in.

YAWK IT UP

You pause in the woods and hear strange turkey talk. It's far from the melodious calling of a hen, but it doesn't really sound like a mature tom's slow-cadenced yelping. The single and double notes are more like . . . croaks?

Sit down quickly against the nearest tree and prepare to call. Love-starved jakes that travel with a dominant gobbler in the spring often yawk it up each time the big boy struts for hens. Try your own brand of yawking to lure the inquisitive young gobblers. They might bring in tow a silent longbeard you had no idea was strutting in the area. The oddball call is easiest to mimic on a mouth diaphragm, especially a stack-frame model. Huff air up from your chest and pop it over the rubber reeds while actually saying "yawk." Cut off your single or double notes abruptly to achieve that awful croaking sound.

POWER PLAY

When a creek, ditch or fence hangs up a gobbler, it's always best to maneuver around and take the obstacle out of play. But what if a tom struts on an open knoll overlooking a deep gully? Or what can you do when a bird gobbles his fool head off on the opposite side of a stream too deep to wade? Sometimes you just gotta try to call a turkey across a hazard.

Hit a stonewalled bird with a burst of loud, excited yelping and cutting. Then, lay down your calls and *keep your hands off them* for 10 to 20 minutes. A tom in peak breeding mode may strut back and forth along the hazard, gobbling like a banshee. If real hens fail to show, however, he might just do the improbable and fly the hazard in search of the hot girl who has mysteriously clammed up.

COY TOY

You've been yelping awhile and a tom is firing back gobbles as he closes within 80, 70, 60 yards of your setup tree. Stop calling! That bird is searching for the "hen," so give him time to work. If you float just one more cluck, yelp or purr, a tight tom might do what comes naturally: Stop, explode into strut and wait for his love interest to come the rest of the way to him.

Ah, but if a gobbler throws on the brakes and hangs up tantalizingly close, say 50 steps out, you need to coax him closer. What then? Cluck and purr ever so softly when the bird stirs his feet in the leaves, vibrates his wings while strutting or runs out his neck to gobble. Anytime a tom moves some part of his anatomy, his hearing is less acute, and there is a smaller chance that he'll pinpoint the location of your calls. The bird will have to take a few more steps in search of the sweet-talking hen, and he might just drift within range of your shotgun.

GET THE DROP ON HIM

You hunt the same turkey three mornings in a row. Each day he roars at your hen calls, but when he pitches from the roost he hangs up or simply marches away with a bevy of hens. You've tried circling him and dogging him—nothing. You're down to desperate measures.

Dawn of the fourth day: Wait for the gobbler to fly down from his roost (the thumping of heavy wings followed by a foliage-muffled gobble tells you the tom is on the ground), then hit him with a booming gobble from a tube call or rubber shaker.

The gobbler will do a double take, wondering—if turkeys do indeed wonder—something along the lines of "Who the %$#&* has the gall to invade my breeding turf!" In all likelihood, the bird will bellow an agitated gobble in an effort to suppress you with his dominance. Gobble right back and let him know you're here to stay. At that point the turkey might run over to kick some butt feathers, only to have the tables turned on him. (A safety note: Never challenge a tom with gobbling on private or public land that receives even moderate hunting pressure. Fake gobbles can draw other hunters into your area.)

WHINING ALLOWED

It's a good bet that many of the toms you'll encounter this spring will be surrounded by harems of hens. Even as you work the gobblers, be sure to pay attention to the calling of the ladies. Many hens are pure yelpers—their *kee-awks* either trilling or raspy—but some girls toss short whines, squeals and squeaks into their yelping sequences.

If you listen closely, you'll hear these audible idiosyncrasies that drive some toms crazy, eliciting booming gobbles and intense drumming. It stands to reason that tweaking your own yelping in similar fashion can have the same effect.

DIAPHRAGM CALLS: Amid a series of yelps, tongue-press the call to the roof of your mouth for a split second, then resume the sequence. The break will result in a subtle squeal.

BOX CALLS: Pull the handle an inch sideways, press it firmly to the sounding lip and make a tight, whiny stroke before running a yelping sequence.

PEG-AND-POT FRICTION CALL: Tighten finger pressure on the striker and stroke it hard against the slate, glass or aluminum surface for an instant while yelping. The resulting squeaks and squeals may cause a tom to rip gobbles and commit your way.

VENTRILOQUISM

A turkey hen is a feathery bundle of nervous energy, walking the spring woods with a herky-jerky gait, fidgeting as she clucks, yelps and purrs. You can play off a hen's neuroses by floating your fake calls all over the place, becoming a sweet-talking Paul Winchell to keep a gobbler on the move and guessing where you are. He may eventually drift close to your setup tree, craning his gaudy neck and ivory head in search of the imaginary gal that is stirring about and playing hard to get.

With a diaphragm call, practice yelping out of the comers of your mouth, until you can cast calls left and right as well as out front. If you're convinced a tom is standing in a spot where he can't bust you, cup a camouflaged hand to your mouth and bounce calls off your palm while turning your head slowly from side to side (as you've doubtless seen in hunting videos).

Hold a box or slate call to one side of your body and work it there. Then move the call into your lap and scratch a couple of yelps and clucks out front. Then direct a little sweet talk to the opposite side of your setup. Varying not only the line but also the volume and intensity of your calls enhances the auditory magic act.

If a stubborn gobbler hangs up in the brush 75 to 100 yards away, slip back 20 to 40 yards, yelping and clucking as you go. Move left and right, casting your calls all the while you're repositioning against a tree. The tom may perceive your float calls to be a fidgety hen losing interest and walking away. He might break strut and come to cut her off—inadvertently sticking his brain stem in line with your shotgun barrel.

BUSTED IN BED

You're easing through the predawn woods when heavy wingbeats erupt directly overhead, thrashing the treetops. Probably a gobbler. You cuss and throw down your camo cap, thinking your hunt is over. Or is it?

Wild turkeys have amazing eyesight in daylight but poor night vision, so they don't fly very far when they're bumped from their limbs in the dark—maybe a couple hundred yards or so to another tree.

Move 75 to 100 yards in the direction the gobbler flushed, set up, *but don't call.* That bird may sit in his new tree until well after sunrise, and if he gobbles at all, it'll only be half-hearted. Wait until you hear him hit the ground, then call to the bird. Don't be too aggressive at first. Try seductive clucking, yelping and purring on a diaphragm or slate call. Wild turkeys have small brains and short memories. In time, a hot tom may forget about the roost disturbance and crank up his gobbling again—turning a potentially busted hunt into a thrilling morning.

⋙◈⋘

FAKE AND TAKE TURKEYS

by Kathy Etling

HUNTING TIPS AND SETUPS THAT WILL HELP YOU TAKE TURKEYS WITH DECOYS.

ONE OF THE GREAT FASCINATIONS with turkey hunting is the ability to "speak" with the birds. Wild turkeys are social creatures, and they communicate with each other using a wide assortment of sounds. That's why they respond well to calling.

Turkeys rely highly on vision, too. They are acutely alert at all times and constantly search for danger. Their sight also helps them find other turkeys. Gobblers can be especially vulnerable to the sight of a hen during mating season. This means that they can be decoyed.

Together, the combination of calling and decoying gives turkey hunters their greatest advantage. The techniques provide a double-barreled strategy for hunters heading into the woods in the spring.

Anyone who's ever hunted turkeys will admit that neither calling nor decoying will work all the time. Still, when everything goes right, decoying can be unbelievable. When things go wrong you may want to kick yourself for ever trying it.

Although I had considered using a decoy for some time I never got around to doing so until two years ago. That April, I discovered the magic of decoying. I watched, mesmerized, as a longbeard alternately ran and strutted to me, oblivious to anything but the bogus hen. I got that gobbler, and he never even knew I was there.

Last year started the same way. Champion caller Walter Parrott enticed a wily old gobbler close to where we were huddled along a fencerow. The bird was behind us, but when he saw our decoys, he ran by us so fast I couldn't get a clear shot. One of our decoys was a jake, and the old longbeard was outraged that this young tom was courting a hen. The gobbler blitzed the decoys and began beating the jake with his wings. When the decoy toppled over, the gobbler leaped back, startled, giving me a chance to shoot.

Deluded into thinking I finally had turkey hunting figured out, I took the two decoys along during the second half of our spring season. I managed to call in another longbeard, but the gobbler took one look at my dekes and realized something was fishy. After strutting in and stopping 60 yards away, the tom took off like a rocket. I made one last desperate call as he ran away, and he gobbled loudly right before he disappeared. So much for my sure thing.

Decoying attracts lovelorn gobblers, but it can also draw curious hens who may scold, purr, preen or dust near the decoy, convinced they've found a new friend. Don't discount the appeal of a wild hen feeding near a decoy. Often it will lure a tom into shooting range.

Decoying is not only effective, it adds a totally new dimension to a sport that's exploded during recent years. You can set out decoys in a number of ways. A single hen decoy is probably the most popular and can be effective in luring jakes or longbeards. If a wise old tom is your goal, you may want to use a "flock" with one or more hen decoys plus a jake decoy. (Caution should be used when using a jake decoy. Please see "Decoy Safety Tips.") The decoys should be placed about three or four feet apart. A flock that includes a jake may be all that's needed to convince a wary gobbler to throw caution to the wind while he's teaching the young upstart (your jake decoy) a lesson.

Safety is of the utmost importance when decoying. Unfortunately, creating the sight and sound of turkeys can lure hunters as well as gobblers. With the proper precautions, decoying is safe. And with the proper setup, decoying can be ultra-effective.

DECOY SAFETY TIPS AND SETUPS

- Be certain decoying is legal where you hunt turkeys.

- Use jake (or any male-imitating) decoys with extreme caution. Hunters will be looking for the telltale beard or red head of a gobbler. Use jake decoys only on private land where you know where other hunters will be, and, prior to hunting, alert them that you will be using decoys.

- Wear hunter orange while walking through your hunting area.

- Decoys should be totally hidden while being transported. Some companies sell hunter orange bags to completely cover decoys.

- Set up in front of a "stand" tree wider than your shoulders. This prevents someone stalking your decoy from behind you and putting you in their line of fire.

- From a seated position, identify a sight line to the front that provides 100 yards of visibility. Set decoys about 20 yards from your position on that line.

- Should you see anyone, call out in a loud clear voice. Their presence has already compromised your location, and a soft voice may confuse them rather than alert them to your presence.

- If you decide to move your decoys after a period of time, before standing up check carefully to be sure that no one is stalking your decoys.

- Utilize landforms for safe decoy placement. For example, place a decoy in front of something no one can see through, like a large mound or hill.

- Wear safety glasses when turkey hunting. A stray pellet may bounce harmlessly off your face, but could be fatal or debilitating if it entered an eye.

BACKSTOP SETUP

Although the hunter does not have a 100-yard line of sight in front of him, which is recommended, this setup is safe. The decoy is placed in front of a hill or other earthen backstop so that anyone on the opposite side will not see the decoy and start stalking it. Hunters' setup trees should always be wider than their shoulders.

FOREST SETUP

When using decoys in a wooded area, position yourself and your decoy so you can see at least 100 yards in front. If another hunter enters the danger zone, call out in a loud, clear voice. Your position will have already been compromised, and a movement, gesture or whistle could create a more dangerous situation.

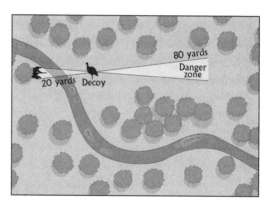

FIELD SETUP

Gobblers love to display in fields, and this type of setup can be safe and effective. Place your decoy about 20 yards away and be sure you have a line of sight that extends at least 100 yards. In a cut field, set up on a wide tree near the fencerow.

Portions of this information developed by the Wild Turkey Hunting Safety Task Force, 429 W. Eighth St., Mishawaka, IN 46544.

CURING GOBBLER HANG-UPS

by John Higley

HAS SOMETHING COME BETWEEN YOU AND YOUR
TOM—A CREEK, A FENCE OR A BRUSH LINE
FOR INSTANCE? FRET NOT. HERE ARE SOME TIPS
YOU CAN USE TO BRIDGE THESE BARRIERS.

THE SHOCK OF THE FIRST GOBBLE almost turned me
inside out. Only the faintest presence of light illuminated the
morning sky, and I was still less than halfway to a favorite listening
point when coyotes had yapped and woke up the limb-clutching Rio
Grande gobbler.

Feeling suddenly exposed on the ranch road, which passed within 150 yards of the tall pine trees where the turkeys were evidently roosting, I backed hastily into the nearest brush line and got ready to call. A short time later, as real daylight gradually spilled over the horizon, I yelped softly with a diaphragm call and listened for the reaction. One tom gobbled, then another and another. Finally, a noisy hen yelped back with the subtlety of a jackhammer. So much for muted tree calls, I thought.

Wriggling into a more comfortable position, I played coy and awaited further developments. One by one the gobblers followed the lead of the hens they could see and flew down from the trees in the opposite direction from where I had set up. One or more toms still answered when I yelped, but they kept moving farther away.

I decided to try to circle the birds and call from another direction. But before I could make the move some of the turkeys launched themselves across a narrow canyon, still moving away from me. At least two of the toms gobbled from the timbered hillside on the other side.

As old-time showman Jimmy Durante used to say, "It was a revolting development." The runoff-fed stream running through the bottom of the canyon was at least 30 feet wide. I could have waded across it, certainly, but I would have been wet to my waist, assuming I didn't slip and take a swim. Frankly, I figured my chances of waylaying one of those toms hovered between slim and none, but it was far too early to give up for the day.

The dilemma was classic, and like everything else involved in turkey hunting, there was no surefire solution. I knew that every move would be a gamble. For one thing, the turkeys might see me from the opposite hillside. For another, it's often difficult to entice a wild turkey across a rope-wide rivulet let alone a thrashing stretch of trout stream. But two decades of turkey hunting had taught me that it sometimes pays to keep trying, and I fully intended to.

A short distance below the rim of the canyon I saw a flat grassy spot with a view of the opposite hillside. It seemed like a good landing area so I set up there next to a tall ponderosa pine. Using a raspy diaphragm call I sent a flurry of yelps across the canyon. Both toms gobbled in response but held their ground. I called, cajoled and pleaded with them for 20 minutes to no avail.

The toms continued to gobble to my calls, indicating that they probably were no longer with any hens, and giving me a tiny glimmer of hope. But because the birds wouldn't come any closer, a move on my part was in order. There was another wide spot by the stream that looked promising. It seemed like a natural route for the toms to take to the water, and I could shoot across the stream if need be. It was worth a try.

Sitting in the alders, I dug out my box call and sent the loudest yelps possible across the noisy stream. A faint gobble told me that the toms heard me. I yelped again and an instant later, both toms were in the air, coming in like jets on a bombing run. One tom sailed directly overhead 40 feet up, his beard dangling in plain view. The other followed and both birds crashed down on the edge of the slope behind me. One was less than 20 yards away when I twisted around and shot him before he got his bearings.

Now I would like to claim that it was something special I did that enticed those toms to cross an imposing natural barrier but, really, it was dumb luck on my part. When the turkeys flew across the creek when leaving their roosts, I'm sure that the pair of toms got separated from the hens. Even though the two were probably subordinate males, they were not above taking advantage of an anxious hen when they heard one. I had just been in the right place at the right time.

Show me a turkey hunter who hasn't been frustrated by a tom reacting to some natural or man-made barrier and I'll show you someone who hasn't spent much time afield. Barriers include a wide array of obstacles that turkeys are reluctant to cross. Included are creeks, gullies, thick brush lines, rock walls, woven-wire fences, open areas, snowbanks, canyons, sloughs and roadways. How to deal with each barrier varies with the situation.

When I called those California toms across the canyon I considered myself very lucky. One thing I had in my favor, however, was the fact that birds in that area were used to flying across the gap almost daily. Because of the steepness of the canyon sides, the stream and the thick cover in the bottom, flying was the only practical way for the birds to get back and forth. Whether or not that really made a difference in their reaction to my calling is unknown. Certainly, getting separated from the hens was an important factor, and perhaps the main one in prompting the toms to come back.

A couple of years ago in the Black Hills of Wyoming, *Outdoor Life's* Hunting Editor Jim Zumbo and I encountered a similar situation

The gobblers were excited by the hunter's calls, but had difficulty crossing the heavy brush. The hunter should either change calling tactics or try to move closer without being seen.

with a different solution. That morning, shortly after daybreak, we listened to what must have been 20 or 30 Merriam's turkeys, including several toms, as they woke up and flew down from the nearby pine trees. We thought we'd call in a tom right off the bat, but our hopes were dashed when every one of the birds suddenly sailed across a rugged, rimrock-filled canyon. We tried all sorts of follow-up calling to no avail, and we even considered giving up after the birds went silent.

Instead, we looked at a topographic map and found a way across the canyon a half-mile to the east. Crossing there, we hunted carefully back along the opposite rim, moving no more than 100 yards between investigative calls because we had no idea where the turkeys were. After an hour or so we heard a gobble just off the rim, whereby Zumbo plopped down against a log and I backed away a few yards and made some yelps with a box call. The tom, a fine 19-pounder with a 9½-inch beard, was practically in Zumbo's lap two minutes later. He didn't miss.

When dealing with barriers there are times when you should wait out a tom and times when you should cross the obstacle to get a better position on a bird. Part of your decision should be based upon some serious contemplation about the situation at hand. For instance, is there a known physical barrier between you? Does the tom seem to be pacing back and forth, or perhaps wandering around in circles? Did he rush partway in after hearing you and then stop suddenly?

There are many variables, of course. Sometimes a gobbling tom simply bumps into or attracts a hen that intercepts him before he gets to you. Perhaps he's used to gobbling and attracting hens to a certain spot, like a strutting zone, so he stops when he gets there, gobbles back at you, and waits. Maybe he's a wary or frightened tom that won't come close to a hen he hears regardless of barriers. Then again maybe he simply doesn't want to get his feet wet by crossing through water, or to get his springtime finery ruffled by flying.

Fences can be a nemesis, or they can be used to the hunter's advantage. Here, broken-down wires offered the gobbler an easy crossing spot.

One of the most common barriers encountered by turkey hunters are woven-wire fences—the type with the small squared-off wire holes. These fences often give wild turkeys fits. When you see a gobbler pacing along a fence you might shake your head at the apparent stupidity of what is supposed to be a smart adversary. Apparently, though, there's nothing in their genetic makeup that prepares most turkeys for see-through blockades. I've watched panicked turkeys literally bounce off a fence before taking wing and popping over the top. I've also seen flocks of turkeys cross fences one bird after the other via a familiar route such as a wooden gate or corner post. Hens going back and forth to their nests, for instance, seem to have certain routes picked out and fences are not a problem for them.

In some situations you can use woven-wire fences to your advantage. By scouting out the fencelines and by setting up correctly, you may be able to use the fences to funnel the birds to you. By the sign around a fence you can often tell if turkeys commonly go under, around, over or through fences in a particular spot. However, if you hear a tom coming, and he stops suddenly and starts pacing, chances are good that he's been stopped by a fenceline If there is sufficient cover available to hide your movement you should at least consider closing the gap, perhaps by moving to the right when the tom is heading left. Take a new position within range of the fence. You may indeed blow it by moving, but if you don't take the chance the odds are that you wouldn't have bagged that tom anyway.

On familiar ground most hunters deal with barriers without giving them a second thought. For instance, if you hear a gobbler sound off on the far side of a familiar slough or swamp, you will routinely get to the other side before setting up to call. In another spot a different hunter will probably treat a known fenceline or canyon the same way, thus removing the obstacle automatically.

However, not all of us are so fortunate as to know every nook and cranny of a particular piece of turkey ground, especially in a new location. The idea, then, is to suspect a problem when a tom starts your way and suddenly stops, and try to decipher what the problem is. Some barriers such as canyons and rivers are obvious, but others such as ditches, fencelines, heavy brush and even coverless fields are more subtle. Sometimes turkeys will cross any of these barriers in a rush to honor your calls, and sometimes they won't move an inch.

Some hunters prefer to stay in one spot for hours, which may be best if the woods are crowded with hunters. The obstacle may only temporarily stop the bird, and patience and clever calling may eventually coax him in. In many situations, however, a gobbler simply will not cross an obstacle to seek the source of the calls. A strategic move may be your only choice. You might even move away from a tom while calling, or you may want to make him anxious by ceasing to call altogether. You might simply change from one type of a call to another to see if a different pitch will have a more seducing effect.

The best bet might be to move and set up close to the barrier or get across to the gobbler's side and pray that he responds to your calls just once more. No one really knows why a particular tom will refuse to cross a barrier on a given day, but everyone knows that they simply won't do so at times. There may not be any pat solutions to this problem, but you may, just may, be able to turn things around— but only if you can make an accurate assessment of the situation in the first place.

DOUBLE-TEAM YOUR GOBBLER

by Bob Gooch

WORKING WITH ANOTHER HUNTER CAN HELP YOU GET YOUR BIRD THIS SEASON.

"I SET WAYNE UP THE FIRST DAY of the season and called in a bird for him," said Sam Nenno.

Why would anyone have to call in a turkey for Wayne Bailey, one of the best wild turkey biologists and hunters in America? He had capped off a career as a turkey biologist with the West Virginia Department of Natural Resources by retiring to North Carolina to help with the restoration program there. He has hunted turkeys all over America. Wayne Bailey can call in his own birds.

Sam Nenno also ranks among America's top turkey hunters. As chief instructor at the famous Penn's Woods Products schools he has taught hundreds of budding hunters the ways of turkeys. He concludes his classroom sessions by taking his students into the Pennsylvania woods to work on live birds—and usually calls in a few to demonstrate what he has been teaching.

You just don't find better turkey hunters than Wayne Bailey and Sam Nenno. So why do they team up to hunt these majestic birds of the forest? Obviously, there are advantages.

Calling in your own bird and taking it with a well-placed load of No. 6 shot is the epitome of spring turkey hunting. Few moments in hunting are more rewarding, but the lone hunter has to overcome a few obstacles. It is said that a wary old gobbler can spot the flick of an eyelid. This may be an exaggeration, but it serves to drive home the importance of being well concealed and absolutely still as the bird is approaching. This becomes difficult when working a box or slate call, and is a major reason why many successful hunters have switched to mouth-blown diaphragm calls. Others simply stop calling once they feel that the bird is headed toward their blind.

This is not to say that one-on-one hunters aren't successful. Thousands of birds are bagged every season by lone hunters. It is an extremely challenging kind of hunting that sends hunters to the woods spring after spring. Teaming up with a fellow hunter, however, can eliminate many of the frustrations that the solitary hunter faces.

Let's break down that two-hunter team and look at the shooter first. He is the fellow whose tag will go on the bird. Calling may require more skill, but the shooter also has a job to do. With someone else doing the calling, he is free to concentrate on being concealed and absolutely still. Assuming he has selected or been set up in a good location, he is all but assured of getting a shot. His hands can remain motionless because there is no reason to move them to work a hand-held call or remove a diaphragm call from his mouth. He can sit there in relative comfort, face mask in place, his hands on his gun and his eyes peeled for the slightest movement that will reveal the approach of a gobbler. He must spot the bird, get his gun into position before the turkey spots him, and deliver a killing head or neck shot.

The caller, on the other hand, must concentrate on the calling. He may or may not carry a gun.

A major advantage the caller has in a team situation is the ability to move. He usually remains far behind the shooter, so there is little risk of spooking the bird.

"Position is of utmost importance," said Nenno. "I try to place the hunter in a spot the bird is likely to inspect, and set up anywhere from 10 feet to 100 yards behind him. I may move right or left, farther away, or uphill or down. It's mostly gut instinct."

Don Mawyer, a successful young turkey guide who puts his clients on birds in the Blue Ridge foothills, also likes to move.

"It's realistic for the caller to move," he said. "Hens don't stand around when they yelp; they move. The gobbler expects that. If I encounter a reluctant old bird, one that refuses to come in, I'll begin moving away from him, creating the impression that the hen has given up and is looking elsewhere for a mate. Often the old tom can't stand that."

Movement of the bird left or right instead of toward the hunter may also dictate the direction in which Mawyer moves.

"Gobblers often walk a more or less straight route to the hen," he said. "I want to call the bird toward the hunter, not around him. So if the bird moves to the right, I'll move to the left, or vice versa. Hopefully, this will bring the bird on a direct path toward the hunter."

Nenno once saw a bird circle so much that the gobbler missed the hunter completely and approached within 10 feet of Sam in his calling position.

"And there I sat with nothing but a hiking stick," he chuckled.

"HENS DON'T STAND AROUND WHEN THEY YELP; THEY MOVE."

Just as the shooter can concentrate on his role, so can the caller concentrate on working the bird to his partner. The caller's hands are not tied up with a gun, and he can use any of the calls he brought with him; in fact, he may use several while working the bird. If he is back far enough from the hunter, he has freedom to move and to use his hands. Mawyer often scratches in the leaves to imitate a turkey moving through the forest.

Teaming up allows the gunner to concentrate on spotting the bird, while the caller focuses on drawing the gobbler in close.

Sometimes the party concept may even be extended to a trio of hunters instead of a pair. In a typical situation, the caller may position two hunters, thereby increasing the chances that the approaching bird will move within range of at least one of them. Or it may be wise to reverse the setup, with two hunters doing the calling for a single shooter. Both may call but, depending on the response and movement of the gobbler, they may alternate.

Mawyer and his father did just that for me one May morning. Don positioned himself behind me and slightly downhill, while his father went to my right and slightly uphill. Don and his father were familiar with that old gobbler, knowing that he had a daily habit of circling the ridge to my right. They reasoned that if Don couldn't call the bird toward me, his father could coax him along the ridge and bring him well within range of my three-inch magnums.

"Gobblers have a habit of hanging back just out of range, say at 50 to 75 yards," said Don. "By simply calling from a fair distance behind your partner, you can reduce that range to 25 to 40 yards."

The gobbler that hangs back is concentrating on the caller, not the shooter. In fact, if the shooter is well concealed, the bird will not be aware of the shooter's presence.

There are other advantages to the team concept. First is the old adage that two heads are better than one. Put any pair of turkey hunters together at the edge of a dawn woods, and they can't help but discuss the likely moves of a gobbling old tom. The product of the combined minds is likely to be a better approach than that of the lone hunter. One hunter may be more familiar with the terrain than the other. One may have unsuccessfully called a particular bird before, and his partner may come up with a more workable approach. One hunter may be a veteran and the other a beginner or less experienced. The possible advantages a team offers are almost unlimited.

I'VE SEEN ONE-ON-ONE HUNTERS GO FOR YEARS WITHOUT BAGGING A TURKEY.

Bag limits on turkeys are usually slim—just one bird per season in many states, and only two in some others. It's possible for a hunter to end his season just a few minutes after sunrise on opening day. The only outlet for the avid turkey hunter is to visit another state. Team hunting, however, can extend that season by allowing the successful hunter to call in birds for his friends.

"That's how I got started in guiding," said Don Mawyer. "It got to the point where I was through soon after the season opened, and then my friends would ask me to call for them. I jumped at the opportunity to spend some more time in the woods."

The demands for Mawyer's calling and hunting expertise became so popular that strangers eventually began contacting him and offering a guide fee. He was soon booked solid for most of the Virginia spring gobbler season.

Although he doesn't guide, Sam Nenno does a lot of calling for fellow hunters. During one recent Pennsylvania season he called in birds for eight successful hunters, and a number of others missed their shots. Sam bagged his own gobbler the first day of the season that year.

Not to be overlooked is the companionship that team hunting offers. In no kind of hunting is that companionship more welcome than when you face the blackness of pre-dawn during the spring turkey season. When that alarm blares, the knowledge that a partner is waiting will quickly dispel the urge to turn over and go back to sleep.

"Hunters can cheer each other up," said Mawyer. "I hate to go into the woods with a pessimistic hunter. If he doesn't think he will be successful, his chances are reduced. Hunters need a positive attitude."

Team hunting offers more pluses than minuses, however. Two hunters working together always stand a greater chance of bagging a spring gobbler.

"I've seen one-on-one hunters go for years without bagging a turkey," said Mawyer. "Then they team up with a friend, and visits to the supermarket for their Thanksgiving bird become a thing of the past."

GOBBLE SHOCKERS

by Thomas Rose

IF AN OLD TURKEY IS DRIVING YOU MAD,
THERE'S ONLY ONE THING TO DO:
GIVE HIM THE SURPRISE OF A LIFETIME.

MATCHING WITS and losing to a creature endowed with a brain the size of a walnut is humbling. No, scratch that. It's *infuriating*, an act of defiant insubordination within the animal kingdom. So if that turkey persists in looking for love in all the wrong places (namely, outside shotgun range), it's time to question the classic hunt—i.e., roost them in the evening, return at daylight, then call that iridescent monarch down the old logging road to your waiting gun.

Sure, like it *ever* works that way. Few have described the hunt-gone-wrong more precisely than Mississippi callmaker Will Primos when he said, "Roosted ain't roasted." When you're ready to even the score, reach ape-arm-deep into your bag of tricks and pull out some of these seldom-employed secrets of excess.

LAST-DITCH EFFORT

To grow a set of trophy spurs and keep them, gobblers have learned that distance is their best defense against predators. Add their penchant for displaying their machismo for the ladies and you've got birds that like to strut their stuff in wide-open spaces. Among the most frustrating to hunt, pasture gobblers present unique challenges that require special deviousness to bring them in.

A gobbler that ignores your calls yet flaunts his sexuality while waiting for real hens to join him is a good candidate for a little coyote cunning. A few years back, I learned a trick from a 'yote with a yen for a turkey dinner. In particular, he had his eye on a boss gobbler that spent his days strutting in the middle of a cow pasture around a salt lick, where the cattle had pawed out a depression about the size of a No. 2 washtub. One morning, I watched, frustrated to the point of bawling, as the tom skidded his wings through the dust of the salt lick just as he had so many times. The old bird gobbled like it was his last day on earth. Pity is, it was.

When the gobbler strutted within a few feet of the salt lick, 35 pounds of fur and snapping jaws exploded from the hole like a Patriot missile after a Scud. Dust and feathers flew for a couple of minutes while the coyote kept a death grip on the gobbler's throat.

PASTURE GOBBLERS—BIRDS IN THE OPEN
THAT IGNORE YOUR CALL
YET FLAUNT THEIR SEXUALITY
WHILE WAITING FOR THE REAL HENS
TO JOIN THEM—ARE PRIME CANDIDATES
FOR A LITTLE COYOTE CUNNING.

Since then, a shovel has been added to my turkey-hunting kit. If you asked a score of veteran turkey hunters whether they have dug—or would dig—a pit blind to settle the score with a tough bird, odds are you'd have to take your shoes off to keep count.

The ever-quotable Will Primos shared another story of a bearded patriarch that didn't want to take his assigned spot in the food chain. This wary bird would sail into the middle of a horse pasture at daylight, strut all day long and wing his way straight back to roost at night. After several unsuccessful duels from the field's edge, Primos noticed a bathtub watering trough the bird walked past each morning on the way to his strut zone and formed a cast-iron plan to undo the tom.

Arriving well before daybreak, Primos flipped the old bathtub over (liberating a few gallons of tadpoles), propped it up on one side and began his vigil from beneath. Will's inventiveness paid off shortly after the sun came up when the tom walked within range of his porcelain ambush.

AQUATIC ASSAULTS

If hiding in a hole isn't low-down enough for you, let's muddy up the issue a bit by adding water. Top guns will go "feet wet" when trying to find flocks of cooperative birds. Some of the best turkey hunting in the country is found in isolated places that are easily, and sometimes only, accessible by water.

An amphibious attack from a bass boat has spelled doom for a number of gobblers over the past several seasons. A few years ago, I spent two hours hiking into a remote spot in the southern Appalachians to find a friendly gobbler. Finally, a bird opened up, and we chatted for the better part of an hour, until a dark cloud entered our relationship.

The stubborn tom closed, then hung up, yo-yoing back and forth along a ridge that ran down to the lake. Just when the tom seemed like he was headed my way, distant hen yelps from the shore drew him away. A shotgun blast on the lower end of the ridge broke the standoff. A victory whoop, followed by the sound of a Johnson 70 firing up, put all the pieces into place.

Since then, a tried-and-true method has taken shape for bagging birds along large bodies of water in rugged terrain. Before dawn, motor into a cove and listen for a few minutes. If a bird doesn't gobble on his own, an owl hooter might get things cranked up. Instead of making a frontal assault, back out of the cove and land in the next cove up the lake. If a ridge runs down to the cove, as is often the case with impoundments in mountainous terrain, follow it along the backside to give yourself a covered approach. A setup at the apex of the ridge where the finger of land joins the surrounding habitat is the best spot to work a bird into range.

BREAK UP THE HEN PARTY

Coffee-shop gobblers—birds that have earned a reputation for flogging every hunter they've met—often do so absentmindedly instead of by intent. Often, a tom won't pay you any attention because he's roosting every night with a flock of hens, so if the gobbler you're after has you mumbling in your mug, stop for a second and look at it from his perspective. Would *you* ever leave a sure thing for some cheap 1-900 talk? Not likely. So how do you get him interested in your offer? Simple, separate him from his ladies.

After conventional methods have failed, bust up the party the evening *before* you plan to hunt. Scattering a flock from its roost is risky business, but it's worked enough times to warrant inclusion in my sack of secrets. By morning, the tom will probably have calmed down enough to get back to the task at hand—breeding. And that's

If a gobbler is ignoring you because he's flocking with a bunch of hens, bust the group off the roost the night before your hunt. By morning, your tom will be looking for love.

where you come in. Calling to a gobbler before his familiar flock of hens distracts him offers a lot of advantages. And by breaking the routine that previously kept him out of harm's way, you may swing the pendulum of success in your favor.

Flushing a flock from its roost the same morning you plan to hunt is a last resort. It's been said many times that calling in a spooked gobbler is nearly impossible. But if it's your last morning to hunt in a particular area and the gobbler you're after has been giving you the cold wing day after day, drastic measures are your last best hope. Although less successful than busting the flock the night before, I've seen it work on enough occasions that I'll consider using it in the future.

BLUE-COLLAR BIRD DOGS

If your schedule will allow it, hunting public land during the week can offer exciting encounters with gobblers that will rival the best in the country. On a workday morning, after the weekend warriors have left the woods, take a cruise at first light with a mug of coffee, and look for places where others have parked to hunt birds they heard sounding off from the roost. Since success rates for the average hunter hover below 20 percent, odds are good that retracing another hunter's steps will put you in contact with more than enough toms to fill your tags over the course of a season.

Just last spring, this turkey hunter put some simple observations to good use. Parked on a bare knob in the middle of a fresh clear-cut, I sat on my tailgate and drained a thermos of coffee listening to a hunter a quarter-mile off work himself into a lather trying to coax a bird into range. He yelped; he cackled; he cutt. He even gobbled, something you won't catch me doing on public land for all the obvious reasons. The game was over after 90 minutes when the tom followed a pair of hens onto private property to scratch in a freshly plowed field. When the tom broke into the opening he quit gobbling and silently strutted for the girls. The poor hunter drove away for work empty-handed.

Before daylight the next morning, I located the bird on the roost and walked away from him, heading toward the plowed field. The gobbler's calls became inaudible when he dropped from his roost into the thick understory. Patience and confidence paid off 45 minutes later when the bird gobbled 100 yards away—300 yards closer than when he started from the roost. Simple yelps from a slate call sealed his fate. A few minutes later the tom was pronounced DOA from an overdose of lead.

Remember: Only unethical persons of questionable pedigree follow other hunters to interfere with an ongoing hunt, but savvy sportsmen come back later to bat cleanup.

Another lesson about public land I learned from the feather masters is that owls and crows don't operate four-wheel-drives. Once again, I would have to take off my shoes to count the number of times I've been in a serious conversation with a longbeard only to have some other hunter provide both of us with an education. The scenario usually goes something like this: The high-pitched roar of Gumbo Mudders drops in pitch as a truck rolls to a stop along a quiet gravel logging road. Twenty seconds of silence is followed by either a hitchhiking barred owl or a crow seeking company. More often than not, a mature tom will crane his neck and watch the road in silence. We wait patiently for the all-clear signal of a cranking motor and Gumbo Mudders whining off into the distance before resuming our talk. A pause of 15 minutes or so is usually enough time to calm both our nerves.

On those days when the turkeys won't talk, holster your calls and scratch in the leaves to imitate the sound of a feeding hen.

CALL-LESS CALLING

Nobody knows why, but every turkey hunter has experienced days when turkeys just won't gobble. Speculation on their silence ranges from changes in barometric pressure to the amount of money in the collection plate last Sunday. On those days when the birds clam up—or if birds where you hunt have learned to flee the sound of a yelping hen—trade your calls for a new set of tricks.

A call-shy Missouri tom taught me a lesson in "tromping" a few years back. After locating a bird that had beaten every hunter who tried, I too was drubbed when I began calling to the bird. Every time I yelped, he would walk 20 yards farther away and gobble. Finally, when he was almost out of hearing, I got up and tried to close the distance. I got closer than I realized: The bird heard me walking in the leaves and gobbled. Caught in the open, I tried to tiptoe to a nearby tree. At each step, he gobbled and came closer. When I finally got seated next to a tree, he was 40 yards out and closing. He stood in the bottom of a ditch just out of sight for 10 minutes, so I reached to my right and scratched in the leaves. On cue, he hopped out of the ditch and gobbled one last time.

Scratching in leaves to attract a gobbler is nothing new, but it's an underutilized trick. If you've stuck with me this far, I've saved what may be the best for last. The ultimate enticers for call-shy gobblers can't be bought in any store. They have to be earned. Cagey old hunters pull out their turkey wings when toms become allergic to normal calls. A bad bird on the roost can be a sucker for the sound of a wing gently stroked on the bark of a tree. He's fooled into believing that it's a hen switching limbs. When it's time for flydown, really let him have it by flapping the wing against the trunk. He's likely to come unglued.

A word of caution: Be especially careful when using a turkey wing because other hunters may confuse you with one of the flock.

Throw some of these tactics at the birds this spring and you may earn your own set of wings.

⋙◈⋘

FOUL-WEATHER TURKEYS

by Jim Zumbo

WHEN THE WEATHER IS AT ITS WORST, THE TURKEY HUNTING CAN OFTEN BE AT ITS BEST.

TEN INCHES OF FRESH SNOW is any hunter's dream, regardless of the game being hunted. The quarry is easier to see, you can read sign in the snow, follow tracks, and if the snow is powdery and dry, you can walk quietly.

All of those factors made me a happy camper when I stepped out into the thick blanket of snow before dawn last April. Donned in white camo, I aimed my pickup down the forest road and, to my delight, discovered that no one had driven the road ahead of me. My headlights swept along the undisturbed forest lane, and for a little while only my tire tracks were etched in the pure white snow.

Though it was almost May, late-spring snowstorms weren't unusual in the region. I was hunting turkeys in Wyoming's Black Hills National Forest, a place I've hunted for the last 15 years.

I drove to a favorite spot, an area where I'd listened to five different turkeys gobbling from a single basin just a year earlier.

My destination was still two miles away, when a huge snowdrift blocked the primitive road I was driving. The old logging road wound its way through some superb turkey country, so I decided to leave the vehicle where it was rather than bust through the drift.

I had just carefully closed my truck door when a turkey gobbled from its roost tree close by. The bird's timing was such that I think he heard the faint click as the door shut.

It was still plenty dark, with shooting light more than a half-hour away, so I cautiously moved through the snowy woods to a place where I could work the bird.

The forest was amazingly silent, and I felt sure that the snow had put a serious damper on gobbling activity. However, turkey populations were up in the Black Hills, even more so than the year before. Several mild winters in a row had boosted bird numbers dramatically. The region was loaded with turkeys, but they were being as quiet as church mice.

As early light filtered into the woods, I waited a bit and tried a series of soft yelps on my cedar box call. Nothing. The gobbler wasn't interested, and I wondered if perhaps he had me pegged. Perhaps he could even see my truck from his perch.

Ten minutes later, a coyote yapped in the distance. The turkey responded immediately with a lusty gobble, and for the first time I pinpointed the bird's location. He was about 150 yards away, high up in a big ponderosa pine. I tried more yelping, but he wouldn't answer. An owl hoot didn't work either. I didn't want to be too aggressive, because the bird no doubt saw my headlights and heard my truck when I drove in earlier that morning.

Presently I heard hens yelping in his direction. The old boy obviously had mates with him, which complicated my plans. I had a unique ace in the hole, however. If the bird wouldn't come to me, I could surely follow his tracks in the fresh snow when he left the roost tree.

I heard the birds fly down a few minutes later, and the gobbler sounded off just after he hit the ground. That was the last time I heard him gobble that morning. More yelps from my call produced nothing.

I waited 10 minutes and headed for the spot where I'd heard him gobble. I was excited because I'd be able to follow the flock. Tracking had to be the quintessence of turkey hunting. Surely, calling in a bird to a shotgun is the pure art of spring hunting, but tracking a bird and catching up and working within shotgun range is, for me, the supreme challenge.

I'd hunted turkeys in snow before but usually where drifts lingered here and there from the previous winter or where fresh snow quickly melted off by midmorning. This hunt was different. Every track in the woods would be steaming hot because it had snowed all night, and the snow wasn't going to melt away for several days. The remoteness of the area I was hunting played an important role in deciding on this hunting technique. I would not recommend tracking turkeys if you're hunting state land in Pennsylvania or New York, for example, but I knew that on this day I was the only hunter in the region. I eased along as carefully as I'd ever done in a lifetime of hunting. All the years of stalking gray squirrels, whitetails, antelope and elk came into play. This was the big pursuit, the ultimate stalk. I felt like I'd been training for this moment most of my life.

Suddenly I saw movement, but it was too late. A hen glared at me 50 yards away. I froze, and she took off at a fast walk. She hadn't completely figured out my identity, thanks to my snow camo, which covered me from head to ankles, including trousers, jacket, hat, face mask and gloves.

Picking up their tracks, I followed until they slowed and resumed scratching and feeding through deep snow. Once more they spotted me first and again they ran off, but they still hadn't flown. Apparently I represented cause for alarm, but not enough to thoroughly spook them.

Four more times I bumped the birds. Each time they ran off, I dogged their tracks, and finally, after a pursuit that covered two miles from where it started, I saw a hen scratching in front of me. She hadn't seen me, and I stood rooted to the spot as solidly as the big ponderosa pine standing a yard away. I waited for her to disappear, and then I moved in.

It was a perfect setup. The birds were feeding on a slope below me and I was on a rise above them. If everything worked, I'd be looking down their eyeballs when I eased over the top.

DON'T FORGET YOUR BOX CALL, AND MAKE YOUR CALLS LOUD.

My gun was shouldered as I took the last and final step. I slowly raised my head, concealing most of me behind the snowy bough of a pine tree, and I saw feeding birds 20 yards away. The gobbler was easy to pick out. I very carefully inched the muzzle toward his head. Slipping off the safety, I squeezed firmly on the trigger. The 12-gauge over/under roared, and my bird was flapping on the ground.

I was mighty pleased with myself. This was my greatest moment in the turkey woods, even more so than when I'd completed my turkey grand slam a couple of years ago.

A few days after my 1991 hunt, John Higley, *Outdoor Life*'s California Editor, hunted the Black Hills with Ron Dube, who outfits in the area and guides turkey hunters. Higley and I took two birds each in the region in 1990 (one each in Wyoming and South Dakota), but Higley didn't score in '91.

Four days of blizzards and wind worked against him. Higley heard a single turkey gobble between storms, but it wouldn't respond to his calls. Higley is a master caller and recently wrote a book on hunting Western turkeys.

The previous year, when we killed two birds each, the weather was perfect. Snow had melted from much of the woods, and the temperature was warm and balmy, with little wind. Even if you tried, you could hardly get out of hearing of a gobbler.

Higley made an interesting observation after his unsuccessful hunt in the snow. "There was no snow in the valleys just a few hundred feet below the forest," he said, "yet the turkeys made no effort to leave the higher elevations ravaged by blizzard after blizzard."

Most spring turkey hunters in the United States won't need to deal with snow. A ripping blizzard fueled by bitterly cold gale-force winds, however, may indeed cause problems.

One year, Ron Dube and I hunted the Black Hills in late April during a couple of beautiful spring days. A front moved in and with it one of the worst late-spring storms to hit the West in history. Dube and I opted to hunt when the storm was just getting going, despite serious weather warnings over the radio. It was one of the all-time dumbest decisions I've ever made while hunting.

The weather advisories were correct; the storm lasted four days and piled drifts 10 feet high, killing tens of thousands of livestock, as well as some people. Dube and I managed to get to his house by 2 A.M. but only after busting through three-foot snowdrifts on major highways that were closed (unbeknown to us). It took 15 hours to get to his house; normally it would take three hours.

We had two encounters with turkeys during the blizzard. When we saw two gobblers walking quickly across an opening through deep snow, I piled out of our vehicle and stalked along their tracks. The birds ran far ahead of me to a cliff and took off, flying to the other side.

An hour later, we spotted a flock of birds huddled under a huge leafless cottonwood tree in a draw. Dube made a stalk on the birds and killed a jake. Because of the swirling snow and roaring wind, Dube was able to approach within 20 yards of the unsuspecting birds.

Famed turkey expert Ray Eye, who recently wrote a superb book on turkey hunting, doesn't believe the presence of snow is a major factor adversely affecting turkey behavior. He cites many seasons in Missouri when hunters faced several inches of snow on the ground, but managed to score well on gobblers.

Rain and wind, however, are universal weather factors that affect hunting everywhere. Eye believes that, without a doubt, a turkey hunter's biggest enemy is the wind. "Ours is a sport that relies mostly on hearing and on being heard," he says, "both of which

Despite an opening day blizzard, the author managed to get his gobbler. Poor spring weather doesn't necessarily mean that you'll have poor hunting, but it does often call for a change in techniques.

become harder in any wind at all. But you can still call turkeys in the wind if you're patient.

"Try to find a place that's out of the wind, like valleys and the windless side of hills," Eye advised.

John Higley agrees. "During windy weather, I'll head for a canyon or basin that offers some protection," he said. "I think turkeys get nervous like deer when the underbrush is moving with the wind. They can't detect danger."

John Phillips, an Alabama outdoor writer who is working on his fourth turkey book, says that hunters don't wait long enough at the calling location on windy days.

"Turkeys and hunters have trouble hearing each other in the wind," Phillips explained. "It may take some time for the gobbler to come in, and many times the hunter doesn't hear him at all. I suggest doubling the time you sit at your calling location."

"When it's windy," Eye advises, "take your time. Don't travel very far between setups, and keep the wind at your back. Don't forget your box call, and make your calls loud. Strain your ears into the wind but don't get discouraged if you don't hear a gobble."

TURKEYS WILL GOBBLE
ALMOST EVERY TIME
THERE'S A CLAP OF THUNDER.

"Be careful of your reaction when you finally do hear a bird responding to your calls," Eye continued. "Because a heavy wind can distort calls, you can never be certain of a tom's exact location until you see him. It also works the other way around. The gobbler may have trouble pinpointing your calls."

John Phillips sees an advantage to hunting in the wind. "Because birds don't detect movement and sounds very well when the wind is blowing," he says, "you can get into closer calling position more readily when they're in openings or along the edges of fields."

Rain is a big problem in turkey woods because, like wind, it cuts down on hearing for both the turkey and the hunter. Turkeys, however, will normally maintain their regular behavior patterns in a rainstorm. As Ray Eye put it, "Turkeys get to play their mating game only a few weeks of the year, and they're not likely to let a little water get in their way. As I see it, neither will most good turkey hunters."

John Phillips has an interesting philosophy regarding rainstorms. "Birds on public land are hammered hard," he explained. "Most hunters stay home on rainy days, relieving pressure on gobblers. Turkeys are rarely disturbed by hunters on rainy days, and that's exactly why I like to hunt them then."

Phillips says that cedar box and slate calls usually don't perform well when they're wet. For that reason, he likes plexiglass/peg or mouth diaphragm calls.

John Higley has a number of semi-wild birds in his backyard where he can observe them constantly. "I've seen them huddle under a tree or brush during heavy rain," he says. "They'll preen themselves after the storm and aren't very responsive to calls until the hard rain quits."

Phillips makes a good point about rainstorms accompanied by thunder. "Turkeys will gobble almost every time there's a clap of thunder," he says, "which gives away the birds' location. Of course, lightning can pose a safety hazard to the hunter, so he or she must use good judgment about staying in the woods or heading for shelter."

Hunters who pass up foul-weather days are missing some excellent opportunities in the turkey woods. Though rain, wind and snow might make the outing uncomfortable, you need to look at it from the perspective that turkeys have nowhere to go during nasty weather. They don't hide in burrows or dens—they're always out there in the woods.

Dress accordingly and accept what nature dishes out, but don't ignore serious snow advisories if you hunt in the North or West where spring blizzards are possible. Lightning storms are another hazard. Good judgment must prevail, despite your enthusiasm to bring home a gobbler.

TURKEYS
AREN'T SUPPOSED
TO DO THAT

by Tom Huggler

COUNT ON TURKEYS PULLING A BRAND-NEW BIT OF TOMFOOLERY JUST WHEN YOU'VE FIGURED THEM OUT.

BOB WOZNIAK FINALLY reached the end of the wooded ridge where two friends told him they had heard a turkey gobble a few days before. Wozniak was unfamiliar with this region of New York's Catskill Mountains, but his friends assured him he couldn't get lost. "Just follow the ridge to the end, and then walk back," one of them said. "We'll meet you here, at the drop-off spot, at noon."

Since the first hint of gray in the Eastern sky, Wozniak had been walking, stopping every few minutes to yelp, but had yet to hear the thunderous gobble that fires every turkey hunter's blood. It was now 11 o'clock and time to turn back; the daily hunting closure was only an hour away.

A thousand feet below him, cars plied a four-lane highway. Across the broad valley and the West Branch of the Delaware River—at least 1½ miles away—lay Pennsylvania and the next forested hill. One last time Wozniak gave out with a series of loud yelps on his diaphragm call. Was that a faint gobble in response or just the slight breeze playing games with the well-tuned ears of a frustrated hunter? Wozniak yelped again, the plaintive notes dying away as the traffic lulled momentarily. Again, the wind brought a barely perceptible gobble. "Each time I called, I could hear him answer," Wozniak would later recall. "Incredible as it seems, it became clear that he was walking down that distant Pennsylvania ridge and heading my way. His gobbles grew louder and more excitable the closer he came."

The gobbling suddenly stopped, and for a depressing 20 minutes Wozniak heard nothing. He switched to a box call and then back to the mouth call. Nothing. Wozniak was ready to pouch his calls for good when the tom suddenly belted out an enormous gobble below him. Here was a turkey with lust blood in his veins, and he demanded to know why this particular hen was playing coy. With seductive soft yelps, clucks and purrs, Wozniak suckered him into range and shot him with only minutes to go until noon.

His friends, who had waited an hour past their appointed rendezvous, admired the 20-pound tom, all right, but doubted Wozniak's story. After they drove him to the Pennsylvania ridge where he had first heard the long-distance tom, Wozniak, who is a pro staffer with Quaker Boy calls, wasn't sure it actually happened either. "I've killed over 100 gobblers in my lifetime," Wozniak said, "but I've never had one do that. Besides running down a thousand-foot-high ridge, that nutty bird had to cross a 150-foot-wide river, a dirt road, set of railroad tracks, chain link fence and a four-lane highway. Then it had to climb the ridge to me."

Turkeys aren't supposed to do that. Are they?

As these remarkable gamebirds expand throughout the country (wild turkeys are now hunted in all 48 contiguous states and Hawaii) and hunters learn more about their behavior, the old myths are fast disappearing. Turkeys *can* be called downhill, for example. They *will* fly across rivers, even those a half-mile across or wider. And they *do* respond to poor calling.

Wild turkeys are so tough and so well-adapted to survive that you have to wonder if there is anything they can't or won't do. Gobblers

have been clocked in level flight at 55 mph, as fast as pheasants. "He hath the use of his long legs so ready," wrote Massachusetts colonist William Wood around 1630, "that he can runne as fast as a Dogge, and flye as well as a Goose." It's true: On the ground a turkey can outsprint most dogs, except perhaps gazehounds, and a scared gobbler can outrun a horse, at least for the first couple of hundred yards.

Not only will turkeys fly across seemingly impossible roadblocks such as rivers and superhighways, but they have also been observed swimming across streams and ponds. In fact, they don't seem to mind water nearly as much as some hunters insist they do. Southern swamp turkeys have been seen stalking the shallows for crayfish, a favored food. The late Roger Latham, who wrote the classic book on turkey hunting, recounts incidents where big gobblers have fought off foxes, coyotes and owls and have even attacked dogs.

Nature has honed well turkeys' survival skills, equipping them with amazing eyesight and incredible hearing—in both instances, many times better than man's. If we could hear as well as a turkey, our ears would be the size of palmetto leaves. But couple their desire to survive with the toms' insatiable sex drive in the spring, and bizarre, libido-driven turkey behavior may become the order of the day.

I had heard about hot-to-trot gobblers tripping over their beards to get at love-ready hens but didn't experience it until several years ago in Massachusetts when my friend George Hamilton fooled a fired-up bachelor into my lap. We had set up a dozen times already that May morning—Hamilton 20 yards or so behind me while I waited, my double-barrel across my knees, a tree as wide as a rhino's butt at my back—without success. By 10 o'clock we were on our way back to camp for breakfast when Hamilton, a master turkey caller who had already filled his tag, had a hunch.

"It's still quiet," he said, "so the call will carry a long way. Let's try here." And with that he swung off the dirt road to park. We eased out of his car, quietly pressed the doors shut, and set up 100 yards into the woods at the edge of a clearing. When Hamilton knew I was ready, he whisper-yelped a few times and then gradually increased the volume on his mouth call. A half-mile or more away a tom thundered back with a triple-gobble.

"He's hot," Hamilton whispered behind me. "Be ready."

The tom flew halfway to us and crossed the road running—how else can I account for the speed at which he came—gobbling all of the way and fast closing the distance between us. Softer and more seductively still, Hamilton clucked and purred. Maybe the bird was a subdominant or had no free hens to service that morning; at any rate, he repeatedly choked on his gobble, and I could hear the rattle in his throat as he ran into the clearing.

LIKE A KAMIKAZE, THE TOM FLEW DOWN OFF HIS ROOST AND LITERALLY CHASED EYE OUT OF THE WOODS.

I first saw him at 50 yards, striding menacingly toward us like some streetcorner thug in a black trench coat. A decent rope swung from his chest as he bobbed left and right like an ebony bowling pin about to tip over. I could see his neon head change from blue to white to red. For a second I was glad I had a gun. Maybe that's why I shot him at 40 yards instead of letting him run over me. He weighed 19 pounds and toted a nine-inch beard. Strange that he didn't display; then again, I never gave him the chance to strut his stuff.

Turkeys that come running like that shatter the myth that all gobblers are hunter-smart and tough to bag. But even those with a death wish don't always end up over a hunter's shoulder because the birds are forever unpredictable and no two hunts are the same. Consider a Massachusetts tom that we nicknamed "the kamikaze" because he had apparently tired of living—or so we thought.

That spring I was hunting with Ray Eye, one of the country's most respected turkey takers. One evening at dark we were owl hooting along a country lane trying to locate roosted birds, when a tom double-gobbled from a hundred yards away.

"Let's mess with his mind a little," Eye said, and proceeded to yelp pleadingly on a box call he had produced. This bird was so wired he pitched off his roost, hit the ground running and raced for us, gobbling nonstop all the way. Not wanting to spook him, we dashed through the woods away from him. "That bird's an absolute kamikaze," Eye panted a few minutes later. "We'll measure his beard in the morning for sure."

Turkeys, and turkey hunters, wake up to a new world every day. There are no certainties. Before dawn, Eye relocated the bird, which had a high-pitched gobble, in a nearby tree. "He's crazy," Eye told Ralph Stuart, another hunter in our group, who had joined Eye that morning. The hunters set up—Stuart, the shooter, in front and Eye doing the calling a few yards behind him. When the tom flew down, he gobbled nonstop, eight or 10 times, on a death march to the hen. *Pssstttt, oooommm.* Stuart could hear the rumble in the tom's chest as the bird spat and drummed. Suddenly, another hunter stepped on the scene, and the kamikaze decided he didn't want to die that morning after all.

That evening, Eye was tuning a mouth call in the same general area when the kamikaze thundered out a gobble. In a repeat of the previous night, he flew down off his roost and literally chased Eye out of the woods. Turkeys like that play on Eye's mind, and he now wanted to tag this bird himself

The next morning the kamikaze was as vocal and randy as ever. Eye quickly got him on the ground and had him coming full strut when suddenly, and without any apparent reason, the bird went silent and hung up. At full daylight Eye found him sitting on a stump in the middle of a field. Eye tried every call in his fannypack and shirt pockets, but that turkey refused to respond. Apparently he just liked to gobble in the dark.

Toms with love on their minds will sometimes go around hurdles such as fences, roads and drainage ditches when they realize that a yelping hen won't come to them. Author John Phillips, who has hunted in several states and has interviewed many of America's best turkey hunters for two books he has written, recounts dozens of anecdotes about oddball things that gobblers do. Once, while Phillips was hunting in Mississippi with J.C. Brown and Allen Jenkins (the latter owns the M. L. Lynch call company), a big tom hung up on the other side of a deep ditch. For an hour this proud bird gobbled his throat raw in disbelief that the hen he had heard yelping from the hunters' blind refused to cross the ditch and be serviced.

Phillips, convinced that the bird would not come in, allowed that he should cross the ditch, circle the turkey and take him on the other side. "No, John," Jenkins argued. "That would be bushwhacking him. If you can't call the turkey to you, no matter what the reason, the turkey wins. You should have to hunt him another day. Be patient and maybe we can bring that gobbler here."

And with that Jenkins and Brown began cutting and calling to the stubborn bird at the same time. The tom, thinking that there were two or three hens now, walked to the end of the ditch and came up through the woods at the end of a field where the hunters waited. At only 30 yards, Phillips shot the bird, which weighted 19 pounds and sported a 10-inch beard.

UNBELIEVABLY, THE GOBBLER BEGAN KICKING AT HIS DEAD PARTNER.

A friend of mine, Al Stewart, was hunting Rios in Kansas one hot morning in May when he heard a faraway gobble echo through the bottomlands below the hill where he was calling. The bird sounded about a mile away, across a rain-swollen creek, brush-choked valley and huge field of grass. But there was no doubt that he had answered the call and was coming. Stewart, who is a wildlife biologist and expert turkey caller, knew that there were too many roadblocks in the gobbler's way to expect him to come the full distance. Beyond the grass field were some small oak woodlots. Stewart reasoned that if he could cross the flooded stream, he might meet the turkey in one of those open woodlots.

Stewart walked 1½ miles to a bridge only to discover that it had flooded out. Luckily, he was able to hitch a ride across the stream with someone who chanced along in a four-wheel-drive vehicle. He then trudged the 1½ miles back to the base of the hill where he had been calling. His gobbler, apparently having flown across the brushy valley and stream, was waiting not 20 yards from the spot where Stewart had originally called. The daily closure time arrived before Stewart was able to work the bird into shooting range.

Turkeys are so unpredictable that the opposite can just as easily occur. A fired up Michigan bird that Stewart hunted one spring refused to walk 50 feet around a fence. Gobbling nonstop, the tom paced back and forth like a neurotic dog on a chain and kept sticking his head into the wire spaces. That bird never did find his way around the fence.

But long-distance treks are becoming the rule as more and more hunters adopt run-and-gun tactics. The slow, leisurely way of working a bird to your stand that produced for years in the South—where most of the land is privately owned—is gradually giving way to more aggressive techniques of double-team calling, moving while calling and running to get ahead of gobblers going away. These newer, take-it-to-'em tactics have mostly evolved in Northern states where there is more public land and, consequently, increased hunting pressure. Stories of turkeys leading hunters on chases for miles are becoming more common each year. Sometimes, if you really want to prick the spurs on a trophy longbeard, you have to pull out all the stops.

A few springs ago in Massachusetts, Ray Eye and I were hunting public land when we heard a turkey gobble from a hill a half-mile or so behind a quaint New England farmhouse. It was 7:30 in the morning. Hoping to secure hunting permission, we knocked softly at the farmhouse door but no one was home or perhaps they weren't up yet. The people at the neighboring farm were working, but they turned down our courteous request to hunt.

On the walk back to the public land, Eye said, "I guess we'll just have to call that bird to us." Eye, who has hunted all over North America, can make a turkey do anything. Well, almost anything. Over the next three hours he coaxed that gobbler down out of the hills, across a verdant pasture and sprawling field behind the farmhouse all of the way to the wooded road edge. Through binoculars we watched the progress of this strutting and gobbling tom, which we estimated at more than 20 pounds with a beard dangling like a black ruler. When he displayed, he looked like a black potbellied stove. Through binoculars he appeared to walk with the jerkiness of a mechanical monster in a horror film.

But he hung up at the road edge, refusing to cross despite my partner's every plaintive effort. Eye tried raspy and sweet sounds, "happy" cutting, gobbling, kee-kees, purrs, clucks and cackles on a half-dozen mouth calls, glass and slate calls with pegs of every description. Even his box call failed. This master turkey would fan, strut and gobble again and again, but nothing could make him cross the road. At 10:30 a school bus rumbling by spooked the bird. We watched him recross the fields, gobbling all of the way, and disappear into the wooded hills where we had first heard him. I looked at my watch. The daily closure of 11 A.M. was minutes away. "We'll never get him now," I told Eye. "He's the King of Reed's Hill, and he's now a seed bird."

Eye didn't say anything, but I had seen that determined look on his face before. Back at camp he studied topographic maps and a plat book of the area. Eventually, he found what he was looking for: access to the hills via public land. That evening he roosted the gobbler a half-mile off state property. The next morning, after stumbling across several hollows and ridges in the dark, he called the tom onto public land and shot him at daybreak.

IF TURKEYS ARE SO SMART, WHY DO THEY DO THAT?

Some of the things that turkeys do, such as gobbling at the squeak of a playground teeter-totter or the bad brakes on a truck, defy explanation. A few years ago an adult bird brought to the pathology lab at the Michigan Department of Natural Resources had died from overeating burdock. Hundreds of the rough seed heads were matted together in the turkey's crop, which bulged like two fists pressed together. Incidentally, burdock is a noxious weed that grows everywhere. You'd think a turkey would know better than to eat the stuff.

Having heard many stories of hunters calling in a second gobbler to the same spot where a bird has just been killed makes me wonder: If turkeys are so smart, why do they do that? John Phillips believes that, like thunder, the noise of a shotgun blast does not necessarily frighten turkeys, but then Phillips has never heard a tom gobble after a gun went off. However, while hunting Rios with Preston Pittman in the Texas Panhandle, Phillips witnessed something even more off the wall. When Pittman lured a pair of boss gobblers into range, Phillips shot one of the birds. The other ran off about 75 yards and stopped. Unbelievably, Pittman called the bird back. What was really strange, though, was that the gobbler began repeatedly kicking at his dead partner. Pittman shot this bird, which like Phillip's prize weighed 22 pounds and toted a 10-inch beard and 1½-inch spurs.

Turkeys are the toughest gamebirds to kill. A few years ago when Michigan hunters were required to record their gobblers with the DNR, Al Stewart was working the check station near Baldwin. Some hunters brought in a big tom they had tagged and placed in their car trunk. When the trunk came open for inspection, the bird stood up and flew away. Someone bagging that gobbler for the second time might well have wondered how the bird attached the kill tag to his own leg. After all, turkeys aren't supposed to do that. Are they?

—◆—

SULTAN
OF THE
SWAMP

by H. Lea Lawrence

SOME TURKEY TALK IS ALMOST INAUDIBLE, EVEN AT
CLOSE RANGE. IF YOU CAN WHISPER THESE SWEET
NOTHINGS, YOU HAVE A CHANCE TO SCORE.

WHEN PAUL BUTSKI LOWERED his compact binoculars and
shrugged, I knew what was coming.

"He's done it again—walked away with his harem without even a
look back," Paul whispered. "That's the most cautious gobbler I've
ever hunted."

I began limbering up after nearly an hour of remaining stone-still and
enduring the torture of cramping muscles, itches and the constant
cloud of mosquitoes and gnats before my eyes. I received the bad
news with both regret and relief. At least the discomfort was over.

This was the third straight morning of drama with the same conclusion, and I was beginning to think that perhaps we'd better seek a less sophisticated quarry.

I was beginning to feel a bit sorry for Paul, too. He'd been trying to figure out this particular bird for quite a while, and nothing seemed to work.

Paul is one of the best turkey callers in the nation. He won the Grand National Championship in 1985 and 1986, and both the 1985 U.S. Open and the 1985 Levi Garrett Open. These wins are points of pride, but his performance on the real thing is what is most important to him.

"This is my sixth straight strikeout with this gobbler," Paul told me, "but seven is a lucky number, so maybe tomorrow will be our lucky day."

He said it without apparent enthusiasm, and I understood his mood. The worrisome turkey was getting to him. Paul called the gobbler "The Swamp Sultan," which seemed very appropriate.

"He's the head gobbler in these parts," Paul explained, "and no doubt he has the choice of hens. He's a monarch with a bevy of beauties, but even monarchs are vulnerable, and I'm going to get him one way or another.

"All gobblers are vulnerable in one way or another," Paul went on, "and I think that we may be able to go to him instead of having him come to us. I've approached plenty of gobblers by letting them do almost all of the talking. That gives me the chance to get close, which might not be possible otherwise. And we'll try it tomorrow before full light."

Sunlight was filtering down through the new leaves and creating only a dim green glow in the lush spring vegetation of the marshy bottomland. The wisps of mist that had slowly snaked through the trees at daybreak had vanished, and the bold sounds of early morning—the chilling *ooo-wahs* of barred owls and the coarse banter of awakening crows—had faded. Now, we heard the jumbled notes of a variety of songbirds that flitted through the trees above us.

From far away I heard a turkey gobble, and after a minute or so, a shotgun blast.

"That's Jim," Paul said with a grin as we walked out of the swamp.

"That bird outfoxed him yesterday, and he said he'd try again this morning. Sounds like he succeeded."

He was referring to Jim Morgan, who, along with Dave Lyon and George Elijah, owns Southern Sportsman Lodge, a turkey and deer hunting operation in south-central Alabama near Hayneville, midway between Montgomery and Selma. With close to 20,000 acres of prime hunting land, a modern lodge with superb Southern cooking, and experienced guides, it's one of the best operations of its kind in the South. Additionally, Lowndes County, in which it is located, is one of the best counties for turkey and whitetail deer hunting in the nation. Paul, a native of Niagara Falls, New York, is a friend of the owners, and he spends time with them every spring, hunting and guiding.

The bottomland swamp in which we were hunting was typical of many in the southern portions of several of the top turkey states in the Gulf Coast region—Alabama, Mississippi and Louisiana in particular. The slow, meandering waterways create areas of marshy ground with lush vegetation and stands of hardwood timber that include many mast-producing species such as oak, hickory and pecan. This is ideal turkey habitat, and though it's usually more difficult to hunt in these swamps than on higher ground, it can be much more productive. There are also small cypress swamps— isolated bits of prime habitat that are favored by turkeys. I've hunted many of them in southwestern Alabama.

Turkeys like these swamps because they provide abundant food and protection from predators, man included. Experienced turkey hunters also know that the birds like to roost over water. In the swamp where we were, a few days of heavy rain the preceding week had poured more water on the ground than it could absorb, and the sluggish, meandering stream that looped lazily through the swamp had overflowed. The water had receded, but at the moment the ground was pretty muddy.

The ride to the edge of the swamp the following morning was an eerie experience. We moved along effortlessly without lights in the dim illumination of a half-lidded moon through patches of white mist. The purr of the all-terrain vehicle was subdued, and I knew that it wouldn't disturb wildlife at that early time of day. We crossed a log bridge that had been built especially to accommodate the ATV, and then we left the vehicle. We waited to let the silence settle back into place.

"We're going to move fast and far this morning when he sounds off," Paul whispered. "I doubt that he's crossed the creek, but of course there's always the chance that he has. We may have to do a little wading. The closer we can get before I call, the better chance we have. With the kind of harem he already has, his curiosity about a strange hen isn't strong."

The situation was typical of the time when the old gobblers have gathered up all of the hens they can locate and have become blasé about acquiring more. Earlier, when the mating urge first comes upon them and they begin a frantic search for hens, they're easier to call in. Sometimes, a single yelp will bring them running. Conversely, after the hens have left to nest and the gobblers suddenly find themselves alone, frustration sets in, and the gobblers again respond to calling.

Paul had been able to see The Sultan a few times because the bird seemed to gravitate to a small opening where bright sunlight broke through the trees. The gobbler apparently liked the warmth after a night in the swamp's dampness. Paul is never without his binoculars, and finds them very useful in thick cover where it's often impossible to spot a turkey with the naked eye.

The Sultan's first gobble boomed forth with unexpected volume. Either there was some acoustical trick, or the bird was closer than Paul had supposed.

THERE IS NO GUARANTEE THAT A TURKEY WILL ROOST IN THE SAME TREE FOR ANY LENGTH OF TIME.

"He roosted in a different place," Paul whispered. "He's closer this morning."

There is no guarantee that a turkey will roost in the same tree for any length of time, although it's likely that he will stay in the same general area unless something happens to run him out of his home

Swamp gobblers are much more at home in their water world than hunters.

territory. Birds that survive being shot at or even hit by hunters often desert home grounds for other places, and young gobblers sometimes make raids outside their usual range to find hens when there are slim pickings at home. In this case, Paul sensed that The Sultan was about where he had been the previous day, but slightly nearer us.

There was a slight blush in the eastern sky, and I heard a chorus of cockcrows from far away. Somewhere, a farm dog barked at the last imagined intruders of the night. There was a gentle breeze, soft as pussy willow, and on it rode the heavy fragrance of yellow jasmine and a blend of aromas from other swamp blossoms.

Paul waited for one more outburst from The Sultan, and then we began moving rapidly toward the place where he still held forth from the roost. The understory was mixture of saplings, palmettos, low growth and tall grass, but we were able to glide along quietly because everything was damp. Paul stopped now and then to see whether he could spot roosted birds. We moved in a crouch, trying to cover as much ground as possible. Finally, Paul stopped behind a screen of palmettos and took out a diaphragm call.

"I'll stir him up a little," he whispered, so low that I could hardly hear him. "I heard him fly down out of the tree."

The Sultan didn't reply to Paul's very low calls, and Paul let five minutes pass. Then, The Sultan gobbled again, and another few minutes of silence passed.

The next time Paul called, he put a bit more volume and a little more urgency into it. Still no answer. The gobbler wasn't tempted quite enough. Minutes passed, and then Paul turned his head away from the quarry and produced three quick yelps. That did it. The Sultan double-gobbled twice in rapid succession.

Later that day, after the hunt ended, Paul told me that the double gobbles told him that we had a good chance to take The Sultan. "He couldn't stand the idea of not having all of the hens," Paul said. "By turning my head, I made him think that this hen was heading away from him, so he gobbled. He still needed convincing, though."

From that point on, it was a classic contest. The old gobbler was obviously as wary as turkeys get. I can't remember how many times I've experienced that kind of duel. It is always a tight situation in which one false note or the faulty timing of a call can end the contest.

Then, a slight movement to my right caused me to shift my eyes in that direction, and I found myself looking at a doe that was nibbling tender grass along the stream bank. The deer wasn't aware of my presence. She ambled on and disappeared behind a clump of palmettos. Close by, the dulcet notes of a yellow-billed cuckoo portended the rain, though the forecast is often wrong.

Then, the change began. Paul shifted from the standard hen-turkey vocabulary to an intermittent stream of small sounds that were almost murmurs—subtle whistles, tiny purrs and muted yowls. They were soft and compelling, the kind of turkey talk that a human being must strain to hear. Paul and I hoped that the whispered calls would have the same effect on The Sultan and tempt him to come.

Later, Paul told me about this subtle form of calling. "Many turkey hunters, even experienced ones, haven't heard some of the small sounds that the birds make," he told me. "You can listen to ordinary turkey talk and never pick up some of the really low sounds. But the birds hear them, and these sounds are important in the birds' communications system. I've studied the sounds carefully, in many hours of listening to the birds at close range and also by using an electronic pickup that greatly amplifies sound. It's amazing how much conversation is going on in a flock of turkeys that isn't audible to the human ear, even at short distances. Of course, there's the matter of learning how to duplicate these sounds and finding out when to use them and how much volume is necessary. Naturally, I learned this the hard way. It took several years to develop my technique, and I'm still learning."

I SOMEHOW KNEW THAT THE GOBBLER WAS COMING IN, AND I SUDDENLY FELT THAT I WOULD GET A SHOT.

The Sultan was silent again. This meant that the bird was warily approaching or that he was quietly moving away, just as this gobbler had done repeatedly. I couldn't guess which was the case, but I knew that I had to be alert and ready. I concentrated on the green screen in front of me, waiting for any slight movement. In my mind, I explored every possible angle of approach, hoping for one that came in directly ahead and in line with the direction in which my Remington Model 870 SP was pointing.

By this time, I came close to believing that Paul was making some sounds that I couldn't pick up. A turkey's hearing is vastly better than a human being's. I simply hoped that the message was appealing to The Sultan. I somehow *knew* that the gobbler was coming in, and I suddenly felt that I would get a shot.

Just at that moment, the top of a yellow-flowered plant shuddered. Seconds later, I spotted a dark movement in a tiny opening, and I took a deep breath that I have no recollection of releasing.

When The Sultan appeared, it was almost an anticlimax. I was so ready, and the bird was so close and right where my hopes had placed him, that I pulled the trigger and fired almost without conscious thought. It was all over but the shouting, and I did just that. So did Paul.

⟪◆⟫

WHY WE MISS TURKEYS

by Jim Zumbo

THERE'S NO SUCH THING AS A GUARANTEED GOBBLER. BUT YOU CAN CUT YOUR LOSSES, IF YOU AVOID SOME COMMON SHOOTING MISTAKES.

WHEN YOU THINK ABOUT IT, missing a turkey at 15 to 35 yards seems to be practically impossible when an experienced hunter is squeezing the trigger. After all, turkeys—especially mature gobblers—are big birds, and it's not as if the average shot is at a feathery rocket escaping through the treetops. Yet turkeys are missed every year by sportsmen who are utterly amazed when the birds fly off unscathed.

Nick Seifert, an associate editor at *Outdoor Life*, is a prime example of a skilled hunter who learned the hard way about hitting turkeys. Seifert is a top shot when shooting sporting clays, consistently averaging impressive scores in the high 70s and 80s. Before he went on his first turkey hunt several years ago, Seifert couldn't believe how anyone could miss a turkey with a shotgun.

"How the heck could you possibly miss a standing target at 30 yards," Seifert had asked Executive Editor Gerry Bethge, who'd just returned from a turkey hunt with a sad tale of a miss. Bethge had no good reasons and didn't really understand why he'd missed.

On Seifert's first turkey hunt, however, he found out that taking a standing turkey isn't exactly a piece of cake. He couldn't believe it when the big bird didn't go down at his shotgun's report; it was a clean miss.

"All I can figure is that my shot pattern was above him," Seifert said. "The gobbler was at 35 yards and was perfectly still when I aimed for his eye. At that range, 60 percent of the pattern flies high, 40 percent low. Now I use the wattles as my aiming point."

Since then Seifert has scored on five good gobblers, proof that his corrective measure was right on.

I'm not about to divulge any brand-new information when I say that the turkey's head is always the specific aiming point, but plenty of hunters invariably try a body shot, which is a major mistake. A turkey is a tough bird. Unless a gobbler is instantly—and I mean instantly—delivered a fatal shot to the head, he will escape, carrying with him pellets not likely to be fatal. Even with a broken wing, a turkey can easily outrun you.

I've been fortunate to have hunted with a number of turkey experts, such as Billy McCoy, Murry Burnham, Gary Roberson and others. In every case, those hunters would put Carl Lewis to shame as soon as the shot was fired. A super-fast sprint toward a downed bird is often necessary to ensure that the turkey will not recover and escape.

Consider the size of your target, and you should be impressed. A turkey's vital head and neck zone is about as big as a carpenter's claw hammer, minus the claw. Therein lies the reason for missing: A very small target on an otherwise big bird spells trouble for all but the most accurate shot.

Add to that the inevitable excitement felt when a gobbler approaches. When a tom moves within range of your shotgun, whether he's just sneaking in or fluffed out in all his strutting splendor, you can't help but be tense. A turkey exudes a great deal of charisma, especially if he's gobbling as he approaches. His sudden appearance will likely arouse goose bumps on your skin and do things to your brain and nervous system, much as the sight of antlers on a buck or bull will.

That charisma translates to two other reasons why we miss: a hurried, poorly aimed shot, or a flinch. Both can be traced to excitement at merely seeing the grand bird.

To overcome the poorly aimed shot or a flinch, try to calm yourself. Of course, that's easier said than done. If possible, rest your shotgun on your knee if you're sitting, or over a log or against a tree. Even at 30 yards, hitting that small target offhand may be difficult.

If you do have to shoot offhand, try not to raise your gun until the last second when the turkey's head is behind an object the bird can't see through. Raising your gun earlier could mean a torturous wait while the gobbler works his way within range. This could eventually mean having to shoot with a shaking gun, or being forced to lower the gun at the risk of being spotted.

Shooting at a turkey that's beyond your shotgun's capability is another prime reason for missing a bird. Most skilled hunters won't shoot beyond 35 to 40 yards, and many prefer a bird in at 25 to 30 yards. When you set up at your calling station, look at the landscape around you and determine the outer edge of your range. Don't shoot unless the bird is within that circle.

Outdoor Life Senior Editor Ralph Stuart learned this last lesson the hard way. "It was 11:30 on the last day of the New York season [hunting hours end at noon]," Stuart recalled, "and we'd heard a gobble from the bottom of the hill we were on. I knew it was the gobbler I'd been after all spring, because he had a pattern of crossing over this particular area every morning.

"We set up on a small knob overlooking an open flat, and proceeded to call two hens up the hill to within five yards. The gobbler was behind them, but he wouldn't come that last little way to an opening I had picked out. When the hens started putting and moving off, I panicked. I rushed a shot and the gobbler flew off untouched.

"Now, I'll either take a perfect shot, or no shot at all."

A gobbler that's too close may also end up being missed. Remember that the cone of your shot pattern is much narrower closer to the barrel. A pal of mine who is an expert shot missed a bird at seven yards. The bird bobbed its head just prior to the shot.

A moving bird will require you to patiently hold off on the shot until the turkey either stops or presents a consistent pattern of movement where you can draw a bead as it walks.

To avoid a flinch or poorly aimed shot, do your best to calm yourself, and rest your gun on your knee or a log.

A major mistake made by some turkey hunters is shouldering the gun or moving while the bird's head is in view. A turkey's eyesight is incredibly keen. Chances are excellent that it will spot your movement and take off. If you try to shoot as it flees, you'll likely end up with a smoking barrel and no bird.

I know a couple of hunters who made the mistake of shouldering their shotgun when the gobbler was facing them and strutting. These hunters thought that the bird was so engrossed in its display that it was temporarily off guard. Don't believe it. A gobbler can transform himself from a fully strutting beauty to a sleek racing machine in a split second. The only time you might be able to get away with raising your gun while a tom is strutting is if the bird is facing away from you, with his fan obscuring his head.

Never shoot at a turkey if its head is partially concealed by vegetation. The screening foliage may absorb and deflect your shot pattern, or cause you to aim away from the vital spot.

At times a turkey may present itself during very low-light situations early in the morning and late in the afternoon. State laws differ on the legality of shooting hours. Normally, turkeys are roosted before and after shooting time, but I've seen birds active at the edges of those shooting periods. For safety's sake and to increase your odds of making the best shot possible, you should never pull the trigger if you can't see your target clearly.

EXPERT REASONING

We asked five turkey hunting experts why they think hunters miss birds. Their insights could help you avoid a blown opportunity this spring.

According to Brad Harris of the Lohman game call company, "The biggest problem is judging distance, especially when a gobbler comes in in full strut. A gobbler looks bigger when he's strutting, so he looks closer. And I've seen where hunters have said that a shot was 25 yards, when it was really 40. Because of nerves and anxiousness, they just take shots they shouldn't."

Ray Eye, a game call manufacturer from Hillsboro, Missouri, blames hunter setups for a lot of missed birds. "A lot of hunters will set up in stuff that's too thick to see through, and they end up shooting through too much brush. You've got to think ahead and try to call a turkey to a specific location where you have a shooting lane. Also, try to work it so that when the gobbler first appears, he's already in range; either that, or mentally mark a spot that you won't shoot beyond."

Brewton, Alabama, call manufacturer Eddie Salter believes that one of the biggest reasons for missed birds is that hunters panic and move too much when a gobbler's in close. "Don't try to jump shoot a turkey," Salter said. "Relax and enjoy the bird. Often when a gobbler comes in and stands up on his toes to look for the caller, a hunter will think the bird's about to take off, and he'll try a snap shot. But a tom on his toes will often go into full strut afterward, giving you plenty of time to plan a shot. Just take your time, and don't move too quickly."

Call maker Paul Butski of Niagra Falls, New York, blames unpatterned shotguns for a fair number of misses. "You've got to pattern your gun every year," Butski emphasized. "When you're ducking under limbs or your gun's getting banged around in the back of your pickup, the sights can get knocked out of whack or the barrel even slightly bent. It's important that you always know where your gun's shooting— where the densest part of your pattern is hitting."

Dave Streb of the Quaker Boy call company couldn't agree more. "Say a guy patterned his gun when he bought it four or five years earlier, but then he goes out and buys a box of new loads someone told him about. Different loads shoot differently in different guns. You've got to know how a particular load is shooting in *your* gun."

If you wear a camo head net, be sure you can see through it. If it has eye openings, adjust them, if necessary, so that your peripheral vision isn't blocked. If the head net is designed so that you must look through the material, be sure you can see clearly. Just the same, it may be wise to cut out eye openings with your knife, as a totally unobstructed view may give you those extra few minutes of shooting light.

If the temperature is cold and you're wearing heavy gloves, take the glove off that covers your trigger finger before you shoot, or it might impede your squeeze. Shooting gloves that expose only your trigger finger are a good option.

When I hunt turkeys, I insist on using a three-shot autoloader rather than a double-barreled model, only because I have that all-important third shot. A poorly hit bird that runs off *must* be followed up with a second or third shot to anchor it. Don't think your hit bird will run off and expire, leaving a good blood trail like a deer. It will almost certainly make an escape unless you can immediately stop it in its tracks.

It's no sin to miss a turkey, but there are plenty of ways to make this unpleasant experience a rare happening. If you hunt turkeys enough, sooner or later you'll be at a loss to explain why you botched an otherwise easy shot.

⇒◆⇐

CLOSE-QUARTER TURKEYS

by Gerry Bethge

FORGET THOSE GOBBLING BIRDS.
FALL TURKEYS ARE THE REAL DEAL.

"I HOPE THIS DOESN'T TAKE TOO LONG," I whispered, half-kiddingly, to my turkey hunting mentor Ray Eye. We were in the woods just five minutes and already the 5° November weather had left me with stinging fingertips and toes. I wondered if it would ever get light and, if it did, whether the autumn sun would melt the hoar frost enough to soften our raucous footfalls. "Cornflakes," I quietly giggled, then offered up my best cliché-rattling twang. "Yup, it's like walkin' on one of them thar linoleum floors covered with cornflakes."

"We're in amongst 'em now," Eye said, returning serve with a whispered Ozark drawl. "Let's just set up against that tree there."

Short, exciting hunts—I had come to expect them from Eye, who had called in my very first gobbler back in '85.

I first met Eye while a guest at a southern Missouri riverside turkey hunting camp during the spring of 1984. The stout, bearded king was holding court perched atop a half-rotten picnic tabletop. His subjects, hanging on every word of the turkey gospel according to Ray Eye, were gathered at his feet firing off questions whenever Eye would pause for a breath between sentences. "I was working this bird once . . . " was how they usually began.

I was due to hunt with Eye for the next three days or until I got my bird. I was completely intimidated, never got a turkey and headed back home wondering whether or not he could work his magic on birds far away from his own bailiwick. He eagerly gobbled up an invitation to New England the next season. He roosted a bird the night before the May opener and just 15 minutes after the bird flew down, I was kneeling over my very first spring gobbler.

I resurrected the challenge last fall. Eye often expounded on the excitement of spring calling to fall turkeys. As an Easterner, I was unfamiliar with his techniques and wanted to see for myself. I, too, fell prey to common criticism surrounding an autumn turkey foray.

Generally, there are two fall turkey hunting camps—the break-them-up-call-them-back hunters and those who take birds incidental to deer or other upland game. When compared with calling in a gobbling spring bird, either method falls short in the excitement department. Eye had long ago told me, however, that hunting fall birds using spring tactics is not only effective but exhilarating as well. I was about to understand how right he was.

Daylight would come—the whistling wingbeats of a migrating woodcock sent the message loud and clear. I strained to follow its batlike flight through the treetops but stopped when my eyes fell upon a familiar black blob and then another in the nearby leafless maple. I had seen it all before, but my visual sightings were usually followed by the utterance of some four-letter word frustratingly hurled in the general direction of a flying turkey. In fact, just six months earlier my hunting partner, Rick Story, had taken to calling me the "Roost Buster" after I ruined several opportunities by spooking birds off their roosts. But in the now-gaining light I could

Just as in spring, scouting fall turkey habitat is crucial to hunting success. Often where you find one bird you will find a family flock. Gobblers typically stay in bachelor groups.

tell that what I was staring at just 25 yards away were turkeys and they were sticking around—at least for a little while.

"There's two right there," I whispered to Eye.

"No kidding," he shot back. "What do you think we're sitting here for?" I had long ago gotten used to the man's warped sense of humor.

Without missing a beat, Eye scratched out a series of barely audible peg-and-slate tree yelps. The immediate response from the surrounding treetops confirmed that we were not alone. A cacophony of yelps came from every direction. Some were loud, others soft; there was a distinct cadence to the yelping of the birds

farthest away, while those nearby clucked as if they were almost afraid to be heard. I sat almost disbelievingly, listening to the woods awaken—gun still lying across my lap, unable to catch my breath and afraid that if I did the turkeys roosted nearby would see its vapor stream.

"C'mon, turn around, turn around," Eye whispered, coaxing the two birds in human and then turkey talk. "That's better. Now get down here."

In the tree, I could see the turkeys, now staring at us, false-start their pitch down flight. Rocking back and forth like a beginning high-wire artist, they looked comical. Then, like two butterflies in flight, the birds pitched off in unison. Used to them thundering off in a crash of leaves and branches, the turkeys' rather tranquil hop off their limbs to a spot just 20 yards from my gun barrel startled me.

"Take him, take him," Eye whispered excitedly. "Now, now."

I fiddled with my shotgun's safety for a moment then raised the Mossberg Ulti-Mag and calmly put the front bead on the turkey's neck. It was all over in less than 15 minutes. After the shot, Eye and I sat back to watch and listen to the other birds regroup. Senior Editor Ralph Stuart's gun barked next. Eye had strategically set him up in a location just 100 yards from us, knowing that other turkeys, eager to get back together with the main flock, would pass his way. They did.

Soon, turkeys were pitching out of trees for as far as I could see in the early light. Several birds passed within easy gun range, Keystone Cop-style, in an effort to regroup and get on with their turkey lives. Eye's continued yelps gave them cause to pause yet just a few short minutes after putting my bird down, the only evidence that turkeys had even been in the area were the fresh scratchings in the leaves and the now faint sounds of yelping hens and gobblers.

I know now that my falls have been changed forever. Octobers and Novembers once devoted solely to bowhunting for deer will include turkeys in a big way. Last fall, our group took six birds. All of them were called in springtime style.

HABITAT

Unlike spring birds, family flocks of fall turkeys only have two things on their mind—eating and trying to stay together. Acorns, wild black cherries, beechnuts, corn and soybeans are some favorite fall food sources. If your fall season opens in October and the weather stays mild, you can throw bugs into the mix. But with mast at a minimum last fall, we found our birds among the hardwoods browsing on ash and maple fruits (we called them polly noses or helicopters when we were kids). Fresh scratchings are, of course, the best indication that turkeys are using an area, but I've found that turkeys in the Northeast move a great deal during a day. Scratchings, unless smoking-hot, therefore, don't get me very excited anymore.

Get out to scout—it's crucial! I know dozens of spring gobbler hunters who begin scouting in midwinter in preparation for the season, yet few of these same hunters ever scout for fall birds. I have gained permission to hunt numerous parcels of property in my area. Early scouting trips (in the late summer for the fall season) consist of little more than drive-throughs. As the summer turns to fall, my visual sightings of turkeys become as good as money in the bank. Because fall birds prefer to stay in groups, seeing just a single hen or young-of-the-year bird can lead you to the promised land. Chances are there are more birds nearby. Gobblers, on the other hand, may or may not be grouped with other birds.

CALLS

If there's one most important aspect of turkey calling I've learned over my years of hunting with Ray Eye, Quaker Boy's Dave Streb and other excellent callers, it's to have fun and experiment. Too many hunters in both the spring and fall limit themselves to a specific calling device and type of call. Their rigidness costs them birds. As Eye incessantly tells me, "The birds are just being turkeys. They don't do any one thing or answer any one call all of the time."

Although the kee-kee, for example, is thought of as a fall call, it also works in the spring. Cutting, all the rage with spring hunters over the past few years, can work equally well in the fall. You get the idea.

My turkey hunting vest in October and November is identical to the one used in the spring. I fill it with as many types of calling devices as I can based on the principle of loud and soft. I carry two box calls—a Quaker Boy boat paddle for extra-long range and a Ray Eye

Signature Series box call for medium and close-range calling. My two slate calls are a Hunter's Specialty triple-glass and a simple Eye slate and corncob striker, one of the sweetest-talking slates around. My diaphragms (I carry about five) are Eye 2.5s and Specials. No matter what brands you select (brand loyalty abounds among turkey hunters), think about the loud and soft concept.

CALLING TECHNIQUE

Get in under a flock of birds, sound like the first bird on the ground in the morning and they'll come running—sometimes it's that simple. While Eye worked on the flock of birds last November, Associate Editor Nick Seifert was hunting a favorite ridge several miles away. It was Seifert's first serious fall turkey hunt and being unable to scout the day before, he relied on the only tactic he knew of at the time—which was to move and call springtime-style.

FALL LINEUP

1) EYE ON THE WILD TURKEY BOX CALL A double-sided box is one of my favorites for working birds in either spring or fall. Reproduces hen and gobbler yelps with equal realism. It also provides much-sought-after raspiness.

2) QUAKER BOY BOAT PADDLE BOX CALL I've endured lots of nasty looks and comments for yanking this one out of my turkey vest, but it can't be beat when you need volume while attempting to strike a bird.

3) DIAPHRAGM MOUTH CALL Best kee-kee reproducer of the lot. A good rule of thumb for fall calling is to go down one reed from what you use in spring. If you blow a triple-reed in spring, try a double in fall.

4) EYE CORNCOB SLATE CALL For up-close and personal work, a simple slate is tough to top. Try using different strikers to sound like different birds.

5) HUNTER SPECIALTIES TRIPLE GLASS Can be used for either loud or soft calling if the call's surface is properly roughed up. Bring along lots of sandpaper—the labor intensity is worth it.

It wasn't long before his box call yelps drew a response and he was sighting down on a long-bearded gobbler. There were other gobblers in the group.

The next day, Seifert and I attempted to get on the same group of birds in an effort to call in a longbeard for a buddy. We waited on a lake overlook for the first rays of sunlight to crack the silent darkness. Although owl-hooting from the very same spot during the spring proved effective in locating birds, fall mandated a switch to a box call. My first series brought a response from the far side of the lake and we were off. However, by the time we reached the birds, it was obvious that fly-down time had come and gone. Unable to pinpoint where the birds had been, we followed scratchings through the hardwoods to see where they were going. Another box call series hit pay dirt—gobbler yelps.

SOON, TURKEYS WERE PITCHING OUT OF THE TREETOPS FOR AS FAR AS I COULD SEE IN THE EARLY MORNING LIGHT.

Seifert and I worked the responsive gobbler into shotgun range, but the hummock in front of us hid the bird from view. Unable to see the challenging bird (us), the gobbler quieted down and walked silently away with his two long-bearded buddies. We later saw them run off after giving up on our setup.

These turkey tales serve to illustrate an important point. If you feel confident in your spring hunting and calling capabilities, then you will feel at home in the fall turkey woods, too. If you haven't hunted specifically for turkeys in the fall of the year, you're missing out on an experience that, to me, is far more exciting than spring hunting.

FALL VOCABULARY

Yelp: Still the big-money call. Makes turkeys respond regardless of the season and can be reproduced on all calling devices. If a bird responds to yelping, mimic its cadence until you are certain you've got the turkey hooked. Once the bird(s) is on its way, I like to get more excited with my yelping while mixing in kee-kees and clucks.

Kee-Kee: The rather strange name given to the whistlelike sounds made by young turkeys. Most easily imitated on a thin-reed diaphragm call. The kee-kee, once thought of as strictly a fall call, also works in the spring. I often use the kee-kee as a locating call.

Cluck: Single-syllable call that often indicates contentment. Easily reproduced on all calling devices.

Purr: Also a contentment call. Many hunters swear by purrs and mix them with clucks whether spring or fall hunting.

Gobbler Yelps: Another any-season call that has grown in popularity over the last several years. I have my greatest success in reproducing it with a box call. Sounds like hen yelps that are deeper and more drawn out.

BREAKING UP IS HARD TO DO

Because family flocks of turkeys prefer to stay together, a group of birds that are spooked and dispersed have an inclination to get back together. Often they will gather at the exact spot in which they were scattered. Therefore, for years, hunters would intentionally disperse groups of birds and then wait at the flush point until they returned. It was and still is an effective way of taking fall turkeys. I've used this method with much success several times until I wondered why anyone would intentionally scare off the game they were trying to hunt. Since then, I've found that calling to a flock of birds can be as effective as breaking them up and calling them back. If you're a dedicated flock buster, wait until fly-up time. Once most of the birds have selected their roosts for the evening, walk in among them to scatter the flock. Head back to the same spot the next morning before it gets light and wait for the birds to regroup. Most times, you won't even have to make a call.

FALL TURKEYS FROM SCRATCH

by Kathy Etling

TAKE WHAT YOU'VE LEARNED ABOUT SPRING TURKEY
HUNTING AND FORGET IT, OR MOST OF IT.
THE "KEE" TO FALL GOBBLERS LIES IN UNDERSTANDING,
AND MIMICKING, THE SEASON'S TURKEY TALK.

THE TWO OF US SCRUNCHED LOWER and lower, trying to
disappear into the sandstone rocks behind us. We'd set up in a
narrow canyon choked with scrub oaks and blueberry bushes. The
frantic babble of confused fall turkeys, emitting kee kee runs and lost
calls, seemed to surround us. Thirty minutes before, we'd busted up
the flock in textbook fashion: Run in, yell your heads off and scatter

them. Now we didn't know what to expect, especially because neither of us had ever hunted fall birds before. My daughter, Julie, had the shotgun; I was doing the calling, imitating the pitiful sounds of lost, young turkeys.

As we sat attentively in the cool October afternoon, we imagined we could hear the birds coming with every crunch and rustle of the dry autumn leaves. *Kee kee kee!* The whistle was deafening, and it seemed that a bird was almost on top of us. But suddenly, there was a rush of air from a different direction as wings flapped nearby. I didn't know what to do, but because the turkey had to be close, I froze—except for my eyes. I looked at Julie and noticed that her eyes were wide as saucers as she looked past my head. She began moving her gun upward, then hesitated.

"There's a gobbler on the rock behind you," she hissed, "the one you're leaning against."

She didn't shoot because the bird was only a foot from my head. And as soon as the tom figured out what was going on, he was out of there. The commotion scared the rest of the flock, and they soon drifted off as well.

When it was over, Julie and I were both shaking. I like getting close to wildlife, but this was ridiculous.

"How long was his beard?" I asked.

"About six inches." she replied.

If this was fall turkey hunting, we wanted more of it.

Hunting fall turkeys can be every bit as exciting as hunting gobblers in the spring. In a way, it's quite similar—trying to call in turkeys close enough to shoot with either shotgun or bow.

But in other, significant ways, a fall turkey hunt is different. There are four major characteristics of fall hunting:

• The birds congregate in flocks, so they can be harder to find.

• Their calls have changed from the spring. The lost call, or kee kee run, is unheard of in the spring.

• Gobblers aren't as careless as they are early in the year when raging hormones send them questing for mates.

• There are far fewer hunters in the autumn woods.

These distinctions make mature fall gobblers one of the wariest of autumn birds. (Julie and I had encountered an obvious exception.) Luckily, peepers—the young-of-the-year—are usually much easier to come by and tastier, too.

WHEN IT WAS OVER, JULIE AND I WERE BOTH SHAKING. I LIKE GETTING CLOSE TO WILDLIFE, BUT THIS WAS RIDICULOUS.

In a conservation success story, wild turkeys are now found in all states but Alaska. As recently as a decade ago, the birds were thought to be on the fast road to obscurity, and researchers gave them little hope of adapting to new habitats. With a current total U.S. population of more than 5 million birds, spring seasons are common. Fall seasons for Eastern turkeys are on the rise. Knowing what to expect when the leaves begin to turn may help you enjoy the sport in a new way.

Turkeys are social animals: they seek the company of other turkeys. But as with most observations about wildlife behavior, there are exceptions. In the spring, for example, birds disperse from their fall flocks to mate and rest. Sometimes two or three gobblers may hang out together, but only one does most of the breeding. The other exception is the lone boss gobbler who prefers to keep to himself most of the year. Because of this, he's almost impossible to call in under any circumstances. Such a turkey is said to be "perpetually out of range."

But these are exceptions. By the time autumn rolls around, most turkeys are gathered in flocks. Dr. George Hurst, a professor in the department of wildlife and fisheries at Mississippi State University in Starkville, knows as much about turkeys as anyone in the country. He's conducted studies on almost every aspect of turkey behavior.

"Turkeys enjoy each other's company," Dr. Hurst observed, "but even more than that, a flock can range over more territory than a single bird, so the turkeys generally find more food. And a flock means more eyes for more security—it's easier to watch out for danger.

"Most fall flocks are made up of hens that were unsuccessful nesters the previous spring," he continued, "and that's most of the hens in the woods. During an average year, only about 20 percent of hens successfully raise poults.

"Hens with broods usually join other successful hens and their young in a 'multiple-brood flock.' Unsuccessful hens are almost never allowed to join a multiple-brood flock.

"In September, the hens are getting pretty tired of their male offspring," Dr. Hurst explained. "Young jakes grow so fast that they quickly dominate their sisters—the jennies. And when they try to dominate their mothers as well, the hens kick them out of the flock. No one likes young jakes—the old gobblers don't want them around, either—so they form jake flocks.

"Older gobblers hang out in male flocks. And, of course, there's the old boss gobbler who just wants to be left alone," Hurst concluded.

Hurst advised looking for fall flocks near food sources. "Turkeys will eat hard mast like nuts, soft mast such as berries, insects and agricultural crops," he said.

"Look for scratchings and droppings to determine if turkeys are in an area. The shape of a turkey dropping lets you know what type of flock you're after. J-shaped droppings indicate gobblers about 80 percent of the time."

Having found fall turkeys, how do you hunt them'?

"You simply can't go out in the woods and expect the same kind of action you get in the spring," cautioned Paul Butski, a champion turkey caller and a fine turkey hunter. This six-time U.S. Open Turkey Calling Champion and three-time Grand National Champion lives in New York, a state that's had fall seasons nine years longer than it's had spring seasons. Butski rarely passes up an opportunity to hunt turkeys, so he knows what he's talking about.

"In the spring, turkeys do most of their vocalizing early in the morning," he continued. "In the fall, they may call all day long using many different calls, even gobbles."

Butski believes that the secret to finding fall birds is discovering what they're eating and figuring out their travel patterns. "Their number-one priority is putting on fat for the winter," he said. "And while I don't scout as much as I used to, I know where birds have fed in the past. If the mast crop is normal, they'll probably be using the same areas.

To get close to a big tom, learn what he eats and where he travels.

"When I look for scratchings I'm also looking for clues to the flock. Droppings are important, but from experience I know flocks of hens and juveniles do a lot of scratching over a wide area. Old gobbler flocks usually scratch more towards stumps and the bases of trees. Knowing what kind of turkeys you're after will help you decide what type of calling tactics to use."

The freshest scratchings are those with leaves still settling around the edges—a certain indication that turkeys are close. The next freshest scratchings have completely barren centers. If leaves or nuts are in the center, or if the scratching looks compressed or beaten down around the edges, it's old sign. Even so, start walking slowly and pause occasionally to listen as you move.

A group of fall turkeys can sound as if it's talking—with purrs, clucks and soft yelps. Every now and then a youngster may wander off and start whistling the long, drawn-out lost call. Groups of hens can almost sound angry as they purr.

If Butski can't locate turkeys by listening, he'll set up anyway—near the freshest scratchings he's found. "I call constantly for a minute or so," he said. "I may make three or four kee kee runs, or maybe several series of loud, drawn-out yelps. Then I sit quietly for 10 or 15 minutes before calling for another minute. I'll stay in the same spot for 30 to 45 minutes before moving to a new one. Fall turkeys may not always answer, but they could be working towards you."

Hearing, but not seeing, a flock leaves the fall hunter with a common dilemma: Do you run in and break up the flock or continue to try to call the birds in? "Sometimes it's impossible to break a flock up the way it should be done," Butski noted. "They might be out in a crop field where you can't get close enough to scatter them in different directions. It's also hard to break up flocks in large, open stands of hardwoods. That's why I always call first. If that doesn't work, then I'll try to get myself into position to bust them up.

"The best thing that can happen is when the birds work over a ridge or into a thicket. That's when it's easiest to sneak up on them and jump out, screaming and yelling. You have to really scatter them if you're going to call them back in."

If you do manage to bust up a flock of hens and/or juveniles, including jakes, Butski advises to set up right there. "Wait 20 minutes and then use the kee kee run," he said. "But later in the season, I may not call at all until the flock does. Even hens and juveniles get cautious after being busted up several times."

Sometimes you might not scare the hen far enough away. "If she's doing a lot of yelping nearby, run her off again," he said. "That's to your advantage. You don't want her rounding up the youngsters before you get a shot.

"Another trick is to imitate any calling you might hear. If the birds are kee keeing, then you kee kee; if the hen is making assembly calls—long, loud, insistent yelps—you make them, too. If her calling gets more aggressive, you get aggressive, too—anything to get the youngsters to come to you instead of her.

"If you break up a gobbler flock, your strategy changes," he explained. "Move 100 yards or so from the break site before setting up. Longbeards are so much warier, they're wise to our tricks. If you bust them up, they'll probably want to get back together. But it may take them several hours to do so. They might not even get together until the next day.

"The fall longbeards I've dealt with respond best to conservative calling," Butski said. "That means calling very, very little. After you break them up, don't start calling for an hour. When you do, use old gobbler yelps and maybe some deep clucks. Two or three series of three yelps each should work. Wait an hour and repeat."

Even if you do everything right, you may never see a gobbler. "They usually sneak in quietly," Butski continued, "and watch for 10 or 15 minutes before coming the rest of the way. During that time, if you move at all, they'll see you. But every now and then one fools you and calls like crazy while it trots right in."

An experience I had a few years back illustrates how much work usually goes into bagging a fall gobbler. I was bowhunting for whitetails on our Missouri farm. The wind was blowing hard, and I managed to slip fairly close to a flock of big, old gobblers unnoticed. I didn't know whether to try a shot with my bow, as the birds were farther away than I liked. There they stood, sunning and loafing just below the crest of a ridge. I was hidden in some cedar trees, and I figured that the wind was blowing hard enough that I could probably sneak away as easily as I'd stalked in, get my shotgun, return and bag a tom.

I ran all the way to the house, got my gun and hurried back, but the gobblers were gone. Using what I knew about fall turkeys, however,

I began to walk back and forth over the ridge looking for them. I figured that they hadn't gone far, and I was right. And although I didn't get a shot, I did manage to spook the 10 toms in every direction right at high noon. Now all I had to do was wait.

I sat down at the base of a big tree and did just that. I waited. And waited. Every now and then I'd make two or three deep, raspy yelps on my box call. But by 3:30 I still hadn't seen a thing. I began to nod off. I don't know what woke me, but when I looked up, a longbeard was standing just 30 yards from me.

My gun was on my lap, and I had little chance of getting a shot before he could take off. The tom just stood there, peering everywhere for the buddy he'd heard just a half-hour before. I knew that it was difficult, but I decided to try a shot anyway. I barely moved my gun before the tom catapulted into the sky. I had a chance for a shot, but I passed on it because there were several limbs in the way. Frustrated, I stayed there until dark, but no other birds materialized.

The next morning I went back. I still didn't know where the gobblers were, and by noon, I had pretty much given up. I went back to the house, but late in the afternoon I decided to return to see if the birds had regrouped. I was close to the same spot where I'd broken the gang up when I heard turkey talk coming my way. The only good cover nearby was a shallow ditch. I lay down flat in it and listened as the birds closed in. When I estimated them to be 20 yards away, the turkey sounds—and even worse—the turkeys, stopped. They knew that something was wrong. So I grabbed my gun and rolled as the birds took off. Luckily, one of them flew right over my head. I busted him at about 15 yards, and he dropped almost at my feet. The gobbler had a 10-inch beard and weighed 21 pounds. Persistence, and the suspicion that the birds had gotten back together and were working that ridge again, paid off for me in the end.

Hunting fall turkeys is rarely easy, but acquainting yourself with techniques that are different from those used in the pursuit of spring gobblers will enhance your turkey knowledge.

—⟫◆⟪—

DOGGING TURKEYS

by Larry Mueller

IT'S NOT AS EASY AS SIMPLY TAKING YOUR DOG INTO THE WOODS AND SHOOTING A TURKEY.

RAPID, EXCITED BARKING EXPLODED far uphill, and four turkeys glided down to within shotgun range. Not a gun came up. None were even loaded. In part, it was a safety measure (a chance shot at a bird running through heavy cover can get a valuable turkey dog killed), but mostly it was a matter of adherence to John Byrne's fall hunting ethic: Incidental flybys are not fair-chase challenges.

Fall turkey hunting is a special experience quite unlike spring gobbler hunting. John Byrne, Virginia's premiere turkey dog man, is not shy about expressing his opinion of the differences.

"I will go spring gobbler hunting, but only to be fooling with turkeys," he says. "I'd as soon throw my hat at them as shoot.

"It's a lowdown trick to sucker a lovesick tom with pretty hen talk. That same bait took down King David, Sampson, the strongest man that ever lived, and who knows how many others. To me, a spring kill is a hollow victory. But an old gobbler called to the gun in the fall is a trophy second to none."

It is the way in which Byrne chooses to hunt fall turkeys that sets him apart; specifically, how he uses a technique that best capitalizes on the turkeys' flocking instinct. Young birds (jakes and jennys) remain flocked in family groups and are difficult to call away from flock safety. All day long they're attentive to the purring sounds that say all is well in the feeding flock. Should one bird lose sight of the flock when chasing a grasshopper, it will cluck to say, "I'm here. Where are you?" And the flock is ever alert for those quick, high-pitched putts that signal, "Danger—get out of here!"

If scattered by predator attack, the hens and their young will remain quiet until the threat has passed. But within an hour or so, they'll cautiously call back and forth in an effort to regroup. The young sense that winter survival demands flock membership and a mother hen's experience. The young gobbler *kee-kee-kee-caup-caup, caups* to say that he's lost. His sisters mostly *kee-kee* unless old enough to add *caup* in their cleaner, faster-paced style. The old hen calls them with her lower, slower *caup, caup, caups.* (Because of her importance to the flock, John Byrne will never kill a hen.)

When they are over their springtime lovesickness, even mature fall gobblers hang out in "old boy" flocks. With all that sociable company, they don't respond well to calling.

But if scattered, longbeards can often be called back to the flush site by well-executed, slow-paced, coarse yelps emitted every 30 minutes or so. There's no urgency about reflocking, so rapid, anxious calling will be recognized as bogus.

The hitch for hunters, of course, is trying to get any fall flock scattered so that it will respond to calling. This requires a surprise threat in its midst, and in the open fall woods turkeys almost always hear or see humans coming. Then, as one, the flock sneaks off or flies away. Here's where fall turkey hunting with Byrne and his turkey dogs takes on its most fascinating twist.

"The trick to successful fall turkey hunting was discovered long ago by hunters in the southeastern tier of Virginia counties bordering North Carolina," Byrne says. "The area was flat and was covered

Turkey dog trainer extraordinaire John Byrne relishes autumn days afield with his dogs. Calling up a longbeard in the fall is, for him, the ultimate challenge.

with mature white oak forest. There was very little understory and no ridges for cover that would allow hunters to sneak up on turkeys. But back in the 1800s, they learned that renegade quail dogs—those that busted coveys and chased behind while barking—made excellent 'turkey dogs.'

"Families developed their own strains of flock flushers and guarded them jealously. To my knowledge, the strains all died out when so many families dispersed after World War II."

THE RIGHT STRAIN

Like the old-timers, Byrne realized the advantages of turkey dogs, knew exactly what he wanted and developed his own strain. It also took a lot of perseverance. It wasn't until after years of trying unsuitable dogs that Byrne finally acquired a full-blooded Plott hound bitch that would tree squirrels and flush turkeys. "Inky," as was her name, never came in heat until age 14, but when she finally did Byrne immediately bred her to a neighbor's weak-voiced lemon-and-white pointer.

The offspring were blue with darker blue ticking. Byrne kept the only bitch from the litter and bred her to "Jack," a setter of field-trial stock but whom nobody could train to point. Out of that unpromising mixture came "Junior." And he was the consummate turkey dog. Since then, Byrne has been able to nearly clone Junior's traits onto pups five and six generations later.

Several years ago Pete Clare, owner of Turkey Trot Acres in upstate Candor, New York, heard about Byrne's turkey dogs, and after a visit to Virginia he decided to go into the fall-turkey-hunting-with-turkey-dogs guiding business. At the outset Byrne was a bit suspicious of what he and his dogs might be getting into up North.

STEEPED IN APPALACHIAN TRADITION, FALL TURKEY HUNTING WITH DOGS MAKES ITS WAY UP NORTH AND BEYOND.

"The first time we drove up there," Byrne recalls, "I said, 'John Tyler [Byrne's 31-year-old son, known as JT], pay close attention to Route 81. I think this guy Pete Clare may be running a poultry operation with a clever marketing twist. If he is, we'll be driving right back down Route 81 early tomorrow morning.'"

But Turkey Trot's owner wasn't "raising" turkeys at all. He doesn't have to. The Candor countryside (four hours or so from New York City) is ideal habitat for wild turkeys.

"It's the dairy farms," JT says. "Barns are cleaned daily and manure is spread on fields. Turkeys pick grain out of it when insects are scarce or when there's no mast crop. This area never experiences bird declines because of food shortages." To complete the perfect habitat, the fields are broken by lots of heavily wooded ridges and hollows.

I remembered JT as a high school senior. That was more than a decade ago, and even then he could talk turkey almost as well as his father. He's now a master caller guiding hunters at Turkey Trot.

TURKEY-DOGGING

Currently, 11 states allow fall turkey hunting with dogs—Oregon, Vermont, California, Wyoming, Colorado, North Dakota, Nebraska, Texas, West Virginia, Virginia and New York. Lest you get the idea, however, that you can take any old dog out into the turkey woods this fall and bring home Thanksgiving dinner, think again.

Outdoor Life Field Editor Michael Hanback has owned and hunted with turkey dogs since his childhood and points out that although he has seen a variety of dog species used to hunt turkeys, scent trailing and flushing instincts are crucial for success.

"Remember that most bird dogs are trained to stop and point gamebirds," Hanback says. "A turkey dog has to cover a lot of ground, scent trail a flock of birds and then barrel headlong into it while barking to get them to flush. Then it's got to come back to the flush site to trail the runners and get them airborne. You want a dog that's a big runner, which means that species like beagles aren't a good choice."

When properly trained, turkey dogs will report back after dispersing the birds and sit or lie quietly beside the handler as the turkeys are recalled.

"The dogs will usually hear the turkeys approaching long before you do," Hanback says. "We had one dog whose ears would perk slightly when it heard birds that were coming in. It added to the anticipation because you just knew that something was going to happen soon."

JT was handling the dogs on my New York hunt when the aforementioned barking shattered the autumn day. "Shot," a son from the last litter that Junior sired (with veterinary assistance) when 18 years old, was still dispersing turkeys when we arrived on the scene. On the average, two-thirds of a flock will fly, always downhill, and one-third will sneak off running, always uphill. Like Junior before him, Shot put every last turkey in the air before reporting back. JT released Buck, a six-month-old trainee, to join the fracas.

HOW IT WORKS

If there ever could be such a thing as a gentleman's turkey hunt, this was it. There was no running to get to a gobbling bird before flydown time as in the spring. Nor was it necessary to run into a flock to break up the birds as is typical for fall hunting. Instead, we simply released the dogs into good-looking turkey woods and walked along behind them as they fanned out on a hillside or into a valley in search of turkeys. Once they did, and broke up the birds, it was time for the hunter to show equal skill at calling.

Byrne's turkey dog training begins at three weeks when John gives the puppies their first solid food, all the while kindly saying, "Here, puppies, here." They lick canned dog food from his hand and become bonded to humans as their "alpha wolves." Later, after they've been introduced to turkeys, these wide-ranging, self-starting, almost self-hunting dogs readily return to their masters after a flock bust.

When Shot and Buck reported back, JT stopped midway up the ridge and made a blind from camouflaged netting and brush. JT had killed his bird earlier, so he would call for me.

Before he started calling, JT slid Shot into his camouflaged bag. "That bag was the best lick I ever hit," John Byrne says. "And it all happened because I was so disgusted with Uncle Sam and his taxes. I threw down my pencil, grabbed Junior and drove to the mountain. It was February and cold. The season was out so I couldn't take a gun, and I left so fast that I forgot my calls. Junior did bust a flock, so I tried until sundown to call them by mouth.

"I had on a goose down suit, but poor Junior—wet, cold and shivering—had to lie still right there in the snow and leaves. Something had to be done.

"That night I asked Miss Sue [John's wife] to make Junior a bag. And now these bags are a part of every hunt. They keep the dogs warm, camouflage them from the birds, and signal to the dogs that now they'll probably get the reward of a bird in the mouth. If another hunter objects to his turkey being mauled a bit, I just tell him that 'all of my dogs have been trained to help in plucking the birds.'"

JT began *kee-kee-caup-cauping* on a double-reed diaphragm mouth call designed to imitate that raspy yelp at the end. A chalked paddle on a cedar box furthered the flock illusion and added even more attraction for the young birds.

A jake answered far to our left. Each response came closer. And then he stuck his head up. He was probably thinking that he should be seeing birds and was unwilling to break from cover until he did.

JUST BECAUSE YOU HEAR A BIRD RIGHT IN FRONT OF YOU, DOESN'T MEAN THAT ANOTHER WON'T COME IN FIRST FROM A DIFFERENT DIRECTION.

The elder Byrne was yelping from a blind with his homemade caller made from the wingbones of previously harvested birds. "These calls take on the tonal range of whatever size turkey you make them from—jake, hen or tom," Byrne says. Homemade calls require more artistry to use, but making them draws Byrne even closer to the turkeys he so loves to hunt.

Sitting higher than I was, JT's sharp eyes caught movement. "Straight below us," he whispered.

A moment later, as my gun was inching into position, JT drew another response farther down the ridge. But he whispered no new instructions to me, assuming that the first bird would come into sight at any second. It did, but only for an instant before it was running behind a large tree. That gave me just enough time to finish positioning, and the extra-full screw-in choke placed all pellets above midneck.

JT was elated with "my" success. I wondered why, because he had done the skilled work. "With fall turkey hunting," JT said, "just because you hear a bird right in front of you, doesn't mean that another won't come in first from a different direction. In the spring, the gobbler talking back is on one point of the compass. In the fall, they come in from any of the 360°. I've been pinned down by fall turkeys, wondering which will show up first, and always concerned that I can't swing the gun in the right direction without spooking birds."

John Byrne asked for a wing of my turkey. Several months later, the mail brought four sections of bones—each cut, carved, and reassembled into a wingbone call made by the originator of the world's only true-breeding strain of turkey dog.

I expect my grandson will ponder that call as I often do my grandfather's hunting horn. Hopefully, the Byrne dogs will still be as perfect for the job then as they are now.

DEER TACTICS FOR TURKEYS

by Bruce Brady

FALL TURKEY HUNTING IS MORE OF A
CHALLENGE THAN CALLING THEM IN THE SPRING,
BUT I FOUND A WAY TO TILT THE ODDS IN MY FAVOR.
I HUNT FALL TURKEYS IN MUCH THE SAME WAY
I HUNT WHITETAIL DEER. IT COULD WORK FOR YOU.

IN SPRING, a wild turkey gobbler is one of nature's most splendid creatures. As the days lengthen and his ardor rises, he becomes very vocal and his booming gobbles echo among blooming dogwoods and wild azaleas. It is a time of courtship, and the gobblers are very responsive to the counterfeit hen calls of the hunter.

During the mating season, locating a gobbler is often easy. Simply be afield with the first streaks of dawn and listen for toms to gobble: You can hear them at twilight, too, for they often gobble as they fly up into a roost tree for the night. In the spring a gobbler wants all the world to know he is alive—and available.

But in autumn the wild turkey gobbler is another creature. He is quiet, moody and apprehensive. Long forgotten are the passions of spring that all but drove him to distraction. The territorial imperative that caused him to lay claim to a piece of ground and defend it against all other gobblers has waned. As the leaves begin to turn, he seeks the companionship of other males, preferably in his own age group. Food becomes his primary concern. Something deep inside tells him to take advantage of the abundance of fall foods, for he senses that winter rides on the wind. It is challenging to hunt turkeys at this season.

Several years ago I asked an old-timer what he thought the chief difference was between spring and fall turkey hunting. Rubbing his gray stubble, he studied over my question for several moments, then shifting a cud of tobacco from one cheek to the other, he replied, "Spring turkey are 90 percent callin' and 10 percent huntin', but fall turkey are 90 percent huntin' and 10 percent callin'. "

I have found the old hunter's definitions to be nearly perfect. I have also learned that there exists a marked similarity in the tactics used to hunt deer before the rut and those used to hunt turkeys in the fall.

When any game species is driven by the need to procreate, the hunter has a temporary advantage, for the animal has a single-mindedness of purpose that results in predictable behavior patterns. In the absence of a sex drive, game species are avoiding enemies and meeting their daily requirements for food, water and resting areas, or in the case of turkeys, roosting sites. Unlike deer, turkeys are gregarious in the fall and band together in flocks. Down South, these turkey groups are always called droves.

By late fall when most hunting seasons for turkeys take place, the young toms, called jakes, weigh 10 to 14 pounds and are as large or larger than the adult hen. Conflicts in the pecking order occur and the mother hen drives the jakes away. The young toms form their own flock and quite often join with other jakes, which have received the same treatment. Occasionally young toms are permitted to join a flock of older males that have banded together for the fall and winter.

A drove of adult gobblers moving along together is an impressive sight. One fall I chanced to see 29 gobblers with nine- to 11-inch beards walk single file within 20 yards of my deer stand. It was an unforgettable sight!

Flocks normally segregate by sex, and hen flocks are composed of adults and birds of the year, which are called jennies. Still, a hen flock sometimes contains jakes or an adult tom or two. Flock size varies and winter flocks of Rio Grande turkeys in the Southwest may number several hundred birds, though such numbers are rare. Other subspecies flocks seldom exceed 40 to 50 birds.

Turkey flocks can be found in much the same way populations of deer are found—by scouting areas that contain preferred foods. Remember that summer and winter ranges differ. The flock of turkeys you observed feeding in a field last August has probably moved by the time hunting season arrives. With the coming of colder weather, the varied and abundant plant and insect life in fields has diminished, and turkeys spend more time in woods where mast is available.

Acorns are a preferred mast for all species of wild turkeys. They relish acorns of the white oak group (white oak, post oak, chestnut and several others) and will feed first on these, if available, before turning to acorns of the red oak group (red oak, black oak, blackjack oak and so forth). The size of the annual acorn crop has great bearing on where flocks will winter and how far they will forage each day. In their search for acorns and other preferred foods, turkeys may range from 400 acres to several square miles.

Important fall foods for Eastern turkeys include acorns, beechnuts, pecans, hackberries, cherries, dogwood berries, hawthorn buds, blackgum fruit and even hickory nuts. Grasses and weeds that are consumed include crabgrass seeds, smartweed, wild rye, paspalum, purpletop, panic grass and sheep sorrel. Corn, soybeans, peas, wheat and rye grass seeds left from harvest are readily eaten. Young shoots of winter wheat and rye grass provide greens in winter. The subterranean tubers of chufa or nut grass are relished, as are spring beauty and dog's tooth violet. Turkeys also eat the berries of sumac, poison ivy and honeysuckle.

Rio Grande and Merriam's turkeys will feed on acorns when available, but most foods differ from those eaten by Eastern turkeys. Rio Grande turkeys eat the fruits of skunkberry, hackberry, cedar elm and croton, as well as various grass seeds, insects and green forage.

Merriam's turkeys consume fleshy fruits, ponderosa pine seeds, gama grass blades and seeds, juniper berries, pinyon nuts, acorns and a wide variety of insects.

All turkeys feed on fern fronds, crayfish, salamanders, snails, earthworms and aquatic insects. Tree and shrub buds also are eaten by all subspecies of wild turkeys.

Learning to identify the foods turkeys prefer is a great aid in locating prime habitat. Still, the area must be scouted to determine if it is actually being used by turkeys. It also is important to learn the lay of the land prior to a hunt.

Look for the scratchings of feeding birds. A turkey scrapes away leaves and ground litter first with one foot and then the other, and then steps rearward to pick up any exposed foods. The scratch marks the bird leaves are triangular in shape, 12 to 18 inches long. The apex of the triangle points in the direction the bird was traveling while feeding. The speed of their movements while feeding depends upon the abundance of food. It varies from 100 yards an hour to half a mile an hour. The following day, or several days later, the flock is likely to move through the same area again. If scratchings are fresh, the earth and leaves that the birds raked away will still be moist. Close examination will reveal the marks of toe claws, which are very similar to the marks left by the points of a yard rake.

The first few hours of the day and the last few hours of the afternoon are the two primary feeding periods. Between these times, turkeys often loaf on sunny hillsides, resting and preening. But if food supplies are short, the birds are likely to continue feeding throughout the day.

In addition to scratchings, look closely for tracks, feathers and droppings. Careful examination of a track can reveal the sex of the turkey that made it. This is valuable information in areas where only gobblers may be taken. A gobbler's stride measures from 12 to 14 inches, while a hen's stride is seven to 10 inches. A line drawn between the tips of the outer toes will intersect the outermost pad on the middle toe of a gobbler and the second pad on a hen track. In other words, a gobbler has longer side toes than a hen does. A track with an outside spread of more than 4½ inches and a middle toe width of more than half an inch is a gobbler's. A measurement of 4¼ inches or more from the middle toe claw to the rear of the heel pad also indicates the track was made by a gobbler.

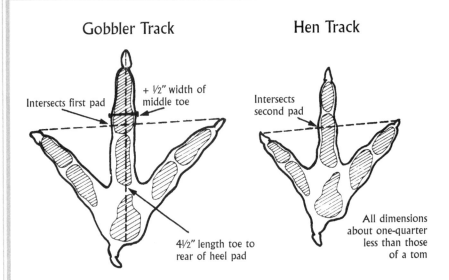

Gobbler Track

Intersects first pad

+ ½" width of middle toe

4½" length toe to rear of heel pad

Hen Track

Intersects second pad

All dimensions about one-quarter less than those of a tom

In many places, only toms are legal in the fall, so when you're tracking, it's important to be able to tell a male's track from a hen's. In addition to the differences shown here, a gobbler's stride measures 12 to 14 inches; a hen's only seven to 10. Droppings also are important. The droppings of both sexes are greenish-white in color when fresh. Male droppings are 10 to 15mm in diameter and the females are about half that. A gobbler's droppings are fairly straight with a finial hook at one end; a hen's are looped, spiral or bulbous.

By hunting season, all turkeys have completed the summer molt and all winter feathers are in place. When scouting, look for feathers as they, too, are an indication of sex. The breast and back feathers of toms are tipped in black, while those of hens are tipped in fulvous brown. Males look much darker than females.

Examine all droppings carefully, for they will indicate not only sex, but also when the birds were in the area. Turkey droppings are greenish-white in color. The brighter the color the fresher the sign. Fresh droppings deposited the same day you find them will be damp and soft to the touch. They dry rapidly, but if dry droppings are broken open and contain a moisture ring, they are no more than two days old. The droppings of a gobbler measure from 10 to 15mm in diameter, while those of a hen are 5 to 8mm. The droppings of a gobbler are relatively straight with a finial hook on one end, like the letter J. Hens' droppings are looped, spiral or bulbous.

Scout for turkey sign in exactly the same way you scout for deer sign. Find an area where deer foods are abundant and you have also located a prime spot for a turkey hunt. Both species share a craving for acorns, and they will feed in the same area at the same time. While deer hunting one afternoon last fall, I positioned myself atop a climbing tree stand that overlooked a creek bottom where several white oaks were dropping their acorns. A scouting trip had revealed scratching, tracks and droppings of both deer and turkeys. A couple of hours before dark, two does moved into the bottom to feed. I sat quietly as they pawed and rooted for acorns in the leaves. I hoped any buck nearby would assume from their natural behavior that everything was on the up and up and would slip in to join the feast. By and by I heard a racket in the leaves more than 100 yards away. Soon 13 young toms crossed the shallow creek in single file and quickly moved beneath the big oaks where they scratched and pecked within five yards of the feeding deer.

SCOUT FOR TURKEY SIGN IN THE SAME WAY YOU SCOUT FOR DEER SIGN.

Deer usually tolerate the presence of turkeys on their feeding grounds, and they seem to know that several pairs of keen turkey eyes will be watching for enemies at all times and that any danger sensed by the turkeys will be quickly communicated.

Feeding turkeys make a considerable noise with their scratching and the racket can be heard from a great distance in quiet woods, particularly along creek bottoms and flats where sound carries well. When hunting deer or turkeys, I depend on my hearing a great deal, and on numerous occasions the step of a buck or tom on dry leaves has betrayed his presence long before I could see him. The stride of a turkey walking through woods sounds surprisingly like that of a man and is much more obvious than that of a deer.

When I observe turkeys moving into and out of feeding areas, I mark the spots in my memory because turkeys are creatures of habit and the flock is likely to appear at the same places in the future. This simplifies the problem of choosing a stand.

I have never hunted fall turkeys from a tree stand, but I have an idea it would be a good way to watch feeding areas. Many times while deer hunting from a tree stand, I have studied turkeys at short range, watching their movements and listening carefully to their calls. In tree stands I have gotten away with movements that would have been instantly seen by turkeys at ground level. Their tolerance of elevated movement may be explained by the fact that bobcats, foxes, coyotes and other predators normally attack at ground level. Even so, elevation does not negate the importance of avoiding movement, for turkeys will often see undue motion even if it occurs 12 feet above ground level. Still, a tree stand provides you with improved visibility and your slow movements are not as quickly seen by the birds.

Hunters taking ground stands should use a blind. I think turkeys have poor depth perception and see images on a relatively flat plane. Still, their vision must be classed as extraordinary. No other game species can detect movement as readily as turkeys can. I like a blind that matches surrounding cover and one that breaks my outline, but one through which I can see.

Fortunately, turkeys have virtually no sense of smell, so wind direction is not a factor in situating a blind. I have had gobblers move directly upwind to within a few feet of my blind. If their sense of smell equaled their amazing eyesight and hearing, it would be all but impossible to kill one.

The idea is to situate your blind within easy gun range of a spot you know turkeys will eventually pass. When successful, this tactic provides a nice sense of satisfaction.

When hunting flocks of turkeys, real expertise with a turkey call is usually of little benefit. Turkeys call to each other in the fall, but they aren't nearly as vocal as in spring. They will often respond to a call, but seldom will they abandon feeding to come to it. Too much calling actually seems to put them on guard, for they sense any turkeys nearby would quickly come forward and join in the feeding activity.

As difficult as it is, it's fun to stalk turkeys in the fall. This is done in much the same way that deer are stalked. I wear camouflage colors from head to foot that match seasonal colors. I smear camo paste on my face. Of course, this would be very dangerous if deer hunting was going on at the same time, but the fall turkey season and the deer season do not overlap in Mississippi, my home state. It's something to think about if both seasons are open at the same time where you hunt.

I like to slip along old logging trails if possible to keep noise level at a minimum. I use the old stop-and-go tactic all whitetail deer hunters know so well. I listen for the sound of scratching turkeys and the calls of a flock in the distance.

As I move along, I make a lost call now and then to provoke an answer from any unseen flocks. The lost call of a young gobbler is one or two flat yelps followed by three or four high pitched *kees*. A young hen yelps more excitedly and follows with 10 to 12 *kees*. This call should have a pleading quality that rises in pitch and volume as it progresses. From time to time I make the deep clucks and the coarse, slow-paced yelps of adult gobblers.

When birds respond, I take advantage of natural cover at hand and try to call the birds into gun range. The idea is to hear or see turkeys before they spot you. If the birds refuse my most dulcet notes, I mark the direction of the flock's movement and attempt to move into a position where the birds will feed into gun range. It is a great challenge to attempt to bag a tom, even a young one, by stalking. Pull it off and you are certainly entitled to bragging rights. Hens are not legal in my state, and it's very important to be able to tell toms from hens, and quickly, too.

A third method for hunting fall turkeys, and very likely the most popular and productive one, involves spooking a flock so badly that the birds flush in different directions. To accomplish this, the hunter jumps up and sprints into the middle of the unsuspecting flock, all the while screaming like a banshee. You must force the birds to take to the air, so empty your gun if necessary. If several of the birds run or fly off in the same direction, go after them again, for they must be scattered if this type of calling is to be effective.

STAY ALERT, FOR OFTEN ADULT BIRDS WILL COME TO YOUR CALLS IN SILENCE.

If the turkeys are well scattered, go directly to the spot where you flushed them, take cover and commence calling. Make lost yelps and *kee-kee* runs. If the birds are young, you will soon hear them calling to each other as they attempt to regroup. Listen carefully to the calls they make and commit them to memory. Make the same calls in reply. Keep your calls going, for you want to give the impression of a turkey too lost and frightened to move.

The time of day has a bearing on the way scattered birds respond. Birds flushed from first light to midmorning are quite vocal and often come quickly. Turkeys flushed at midday take their time and may not attempt to reassemble until late afternoon. A flock scattered in the late afternoon is best hunted the next morning, when the birds will be anxious to regroup.

While older birds feel a need to regroup, they are not as panicked by separation as young ones and may be content for several hours or even a full day. Exercise some patience and listen for infrequent clucks and slow-paced yelps. Stay alert, for often adult birds will come to your calls in silence. A shot may be presented when you least expect it.

I always use a shotgun for turkey hunting. To me the very heart of the sport is to get within short range, whether by stealth or calling, and deliver a lethal load to the head and neck. I use 12-gauge 2¾-inch Magnum loads with No. 6 shot. A scope-sighted rifle greatly extends the range at which turkeys can be taken in the fall when woods are more open and in states where using a rifle for turkeys is legal, but somehow a challenging and important aspect of the sport is sacrificed when turkeys are sniped at long range. I can see some justification for using rifles, however, where fall turkeys are hunted incidentally while hunting other big-game species.

I believe the fall is the toughest time of the year to take an older gobbler, and I get a big kick out of it when I succeed.

A BOY'S FIRST TURKEY

by Ray Eye

"THE ONLY WAY YOU'RE GOING TO LEARN IS TO
GET UP THERE AND DO IT YOURSELF."
GRANDPA'S WORDS ECHOED THROUGH MY 9-YEAR-OLD
EARS LIKE A GOBBLE ON A COLD SPRING MORNING.
THE STORY, HOWEVER, DIDN'T END
UNTIL MORE THAN A DECADE LATER.

MY GRANDFATHER TOOK ONE LAST SIP of coffee, pushed his breakfast plate aside, and stood as he pulled out his pocket watch. "You'd better be going, boy, if you want to kill a turkey," he said, opening the lid of the old timepiece.

His words caught me so off guard that several seconds passed before

I could stammer a reply. "But Pop [as he was always referred to in the Ozarks], aren't you going with me? I've never been turkey hunting before."

"I'd like to, Ray, but you know I've got chores to do," he answered, putting a hand on my shoulder. "Besides, the only way you're really going to learn is to get up there and do it by yourself. Now come on, you'd better get going."

I stood there in a state of shock and watched the old man leave the room to get his old Winchester 97 and a handful of shells. Following him to the back door, I still couldn't believe what was happening.

Just outside the door, he reached up and took down a kerosene lantern, scratched a match against its base, lit it, and handed it to me. "You know where to go on the mountain and what to do, boy. God knows, we've been through it enough," he said, stuffing the shotgun shells into my faded bib overalls. "Just remember what I've told you, and be careful." He placed the shotgun in my other hand and gave me a pat on the back that nudged me on my way.

Holding the lantern high, I headed across the yard, now more scared than excited. Those first few steps that I took as a 9-year-old were the toughest I've ever taken.

Some of my first memories are of the weekends spent on my grandparents' farm deep in the Missouri Ozarks. Located three miles up a valley, or "holler," as they call it in the hills, the farm had been the home of three generations of my family.

The white, two-story farmhouse was typical for the hills. A clear, spring-fed creek ran only a few yards from the front door, near the barn and other outbuildings. The house was set in a rare Ozark meadow, surrounded on three sides by steep evergreen and hardwood-covered hills. The tallest of the hills was simply referred to as "the mountain," being one of the highest points in the state.

In 1962, the year I headed up the mountain that dark morning, most of America was in the middle of rapid modernization. Not so in the back country around the farm. Life had changed little since my dad was born in the house decades before.

Electricity had just made it, but indoor plumbing hadn't, and the telephone never did. The roads were a far cry from what most folks were using. During the spring, the dirt path leading to Grandpa's turned into a muddy trough.

But there were advantages to living such a life. For one thing, it was simple. Everything consisted of hard work and doing the best you could with what was at hand. There was also a closeness shared between family and friends that sometimes slips away with progress.

The primitiveness of the mountains made them sanctuaries for wildlife. Small game was abundant, and deer and turkeys had never been pushed or shot out of the rough back country. Hunting was a part of life. Besides putting food on the table, it provided recreation.

I loved it all, but turkeys held a particular fascination. They seemed to possess an almost mystical quality. They were rarely seen, but they were definitely there. I can remember one spring morning as though it were yesterday. Black storm clouds were marching over the mountain, and Pop and I were hurrying to get the last of the chores done.

With the first rumble of thunder came a gobble from a nearby ridge, and then another and another. I stood there, my mouth hanging open in amazement as the hills around the farm came alive with gobbles. Pop finally snapped me out of my trance, and we made it to the house just as the first of the big raindrops banged down on the tin roof.

Turkeys were constantly on my mind. In the woods, I was always looking for the birds and wanted to know what every piece of sign meant. I badgered poor Pop relentlessly, asking him to retell stories about turkey hunting when he was young. Looking back, he showed a great deal of patience and answered most of my questions to my satisfaction except for one: "When will I be old enough to hunt turkeys?"

"Someday," was his standard answer.

One fall day, his answer changed. The smell of homemade bread was in the air as we cut wood for the cookstove. Pausing to watch me work, Pop smiled and out of the blue said, "Ray, I think you'll be big enough by next spring." He didn't need to explain; I knew exactly what he meant.

A little later, he gave me what became my most prized possession—my own turkey call. Grandpa had made it by hand, using a piece of slate from the chalkboard at an old one-room schoolhouse. For a striker, he'd cut a piece of cedar from a fence post and fitted it in the bottom of a hollowed-out corncob.

The call was my life, and I practiced religiously. Teachers took the call away from me more than once for using it at school. Grandma said I sounded like "a cat caught in a fence," and Pop kept telling me to keep practicing.

The winter of 1961-62 was the longest of my life, but it eventually ended. Turkey season was only a week away when Pop shook me awake one cold April morning and said, "Get up, we're going up on the mountain for a while."

I did my best to keep up with him in the pre-dawn darkness as we crossed the creek, headed across the dew-covered pasture, and found the old trail that would take us up the mountain. We walked along quietly until we came to a huge oak at the junction of two ridges.

I SOUNDED LIKE A CAT CAUGHT IN A FENCE.

I started to ask one of the dozens of questions that were floating in my mind, but Grandpa quickly silenced me with a finger to his lips. He cupped his hands around his mouth and let loose an imitation of a barred owl. A turkey gobbled from down the ridge to the northwest.

We stood there for a while and listened to the sounds of turkeys gobbling from all over the hills. Each time one would call, the bird would rifle back a reply.

As we turned to leave, Pop whispered, "This is the place, boy. You'll want to sit with your back against that big oak, facing down that ridge. Use your call, and whatever you do, don't move until you're ready to come home."

The night before my hunt, I was a bundle of nerves and anticipation. Hoping to make the next day arrive faster, I slipped into bed after supper, dressed in my hunting clothes except for my oversized work jacket and old tennis shoes.

Sleep was hard to come by, and as I lay in bed I listened to the calls of the whippoorwills, the coyotes yipping on the mountain, and the steady sound of the stream flowing nearby. I'd been awake for hours when the smell of homemade biscuits and frying bacon and eggs drifted upstairs.

Normally, I'd have devoured the breakfast set in front of me in a matter of minutes, but not that morning. I picked at the meal and never took my eyes off Grandpa.

When he broke the news that I'd be hunting alone, I was heartbroken. For years I'd pictured us hunting together, and the thought of trying for one of the mountain's phantom birds alone was beyond my young imagination.

I tried to present myself as a man as headed toward the creek. In some ways, it was the realization of a lifelong dream: I was going up on the mountain to try to kill a turkey. The fact that I was carrying Grandpa's favorite shotgun was an accomplishment. But inside, I was as scared as I'd ever been.

With my hands full, I had trouble crossing the stream, and midway across I missed a steppingstone and ended up standing knee-deep in the cold water. I made my way across the pasture, my wet shoes squeaking with every step.

I'd walked the trail to the top of the mountain dozens of times, but never had it seemed so long or so frightening. I finally arrived at the big oak, put out the lantern, and sat down.

I strained my mind to remember everything Grandpa had told me as I quietly slipped the blue paper shells into the pump gun. I sat there shivering from both cold and fear, desperately hoping that Pop would come walking up the trail.

With the reddening of the eastern horizon came the sounds of life in the timber. At first it was just songbirds, and I began to relax a little. Then came the eight-note call of a barred owl. I caught my breath when a turkey gobbled from down the ridge.

I picked up the slate call but couldn't use it. I was afraid—afraid I'd goof up and scare the turkey and ruin my dream. Again and again, I tried to rub the cedar against the slate, but each time I pulled back. Finally, I shut my eyes, swallowed the huge lump in my throat, and shakingly rubbed the peg against the call. I winced at the gosh-awful noise it produced.

Whether it was in response to my call or just coincidence, I'll never know, but the gobbler sounded off. Several more times I tried to force some yelps from the call but couldn't. I finally dropped the call in frustration and clutched the gun that was resting on my knees.

By then, I could hear turkeys gobbling all around me, the closest two being the bird in front of me and a tom on the next ridge. I waited and listened to their gobbling; I could tell they were not moving.

Suddenly, the soft yelps of a hen turkey came from behind me. I began to panic, fearing the hen would call the gobblers away from me. I started to get up to move closer to the hen, but suddenly I remembered Pop saying, "Whatever you do, don't move." Even though it looked hopeless, I stayed.

Soon the three birds were calling almost nonstop, and the two gobblers were heading my way. Then I began to realize that the hen was really a blessing. To get to her, the gobblers would have to walk right past me. Because I was too nervous to call, she was the only hope I had.

I could hear the two toms getting closer to each other, but I wasn't prepared for what came next. From just below the ridge came the loud noises of deep turkey purrs, flapping wings, and feathered bodies thumping together.

I didn't know it at the time, but the two birds were fighting for the hen. I was shaking so hard that I thought for sure the turkeys would see me, and the end of the gun barrel was drawing circles the size of doughnuts.

Hearing the sounds of limbs breaking, I watched as a big turkey rose through the trees and sailed out across the valley. A loud, triumphant gobble came from where the battle had occurred, and the hen rushed back a series of clucks and yelps. My pounding heart went into overdrive. My breathing was hard, and my black-rimmed glasses started to fog.

The next time the tom sounded off, he was so close that I could hear a rattle in his gobble. Like a ghost, he suddenly appeared to my right, head tucked back, feathers puffed out, and wings dragging on the ground.

My first response was to swing the gun and shoot, but in the back of my mind I heard Pop stressing, "Never move a muscle when you can see the turkey's head. If you do, he'll spot you for sure. Remember to aim just for the head."

Seconds seemed like hours, but I waited. When the bird stepped behind a big hickory, I twisted my body, cocked the hammer, and raised the gun. There was a deafening boom as the old gun went off when the turkey stepped back into view. In my haste, I'd tucked the stock under my arm, and the old Winchester had raised up and struck me in the face, bloodying my nose and sending my glasses flying.

Holding onto the gun with one hand, I rummaged through the leaves, found my broken glasses, and poked them onto my face as I ran to where I'd last seen the bird. My foot caught a root, and I tumbled down the ridge. When I finally stopped rolling, I looked up, and there he was, stretched out, his feathers glistening in the sun.

I arrived down at the farm, soaking wet, covered with mud and blood, half-dragging and half-carrying a turkey that weighed half as much as I did. Grandpa heard my shouts and was waiting for me.

He admired the bird, congratulated me, and then laughingly said, "You'd better run along and get yourself cleaned up before your grandma has a fit." I spent the rest of the day telling and retelling him how I'd killed the big gobbler, fibbing a little by telling him how I'd called the bird myself. He smiled and listened to every word.

A lot has changed since then. My life was never the same after I took that turkey. I was in the woods calling every spare minute I had. It cost me girlfriends, it cost me jobs, and it almost got me kicked out of school several times. But it was an addiction I wouldn't have stopped even if I could.

I learned a lot about calling turkeys that April morning, and I've learned a lot since. In fact, I've learned enough to make my living at it. I've guided for more than a decade and am now on the wild turkey pro staff of H.S. Strut, a division of Hunter's Specialties.

Grandpa and Grandma had to move off the farm and into a little community nearby. Grandma's still there and still kids me about sounding like "a cat caught in a fence." We lost Grandpa in 1976.

It wasn't long after his passing that the entire family was gathered at Grandma's. As usual, the talk turned to hunting, and someone brought up the subject of my first turkey. My eyes began to moisten, and I walked over and leaned against the fence to look out toward the mountain that held so many fond memories of Grandpa.

A few seconds later, I felt Grandma's hand softly rub my shoulder as she said, "You're thinking of Pop, aren't you?" Never taking my eyes off the mountain, I bit my lip and nodded my head.

She lovingly moved in beside me and softly said, "Ray, do you remember that hen on the mountain the morning you killed your first turkey?"

I looked at her, swallowed hard, and said, "Yes."

"That wasn't a hen calling behind you," she said. "That was your grandpa."

—⟫◆⟪—

GOBBLER FEVER

by Geoffrey Norman

GEOFFREY NORMAN'S GOT IT AND HE'S PASSING IT ON.

IF YOU ARE GOING TO GO A LITTLE CRAZY, then spring is probably the time to do it. The season has that frantic, urgent feel, what with all the rising sap and cosmic renewal going on. Lovers—young ones especially—have always been partial to the spring, and there are all sorts of outlandish pagan rituals celebrating the arrival of the season. Poets are big fans of spring, of course, and sing its praises pretty much endlessly. Igor Stravinsky's *Le Sacre du Printemps* (The Rites of Spring) is considered one of the masterpieces of modern ballet and it's full of mystical stuff about life and death, including the sacrificing of virgins. Spring, then, is the season for exuberance and madness. A good time to come unglued.

Understanding spring helps enormously if you want to understand turkey hunting and turkey hunters. Not all turkey hunters are crazy;

at least not all the time. Most of them have jobs, debts, ungrateful children. And I doubt one of them has ever sacrificed a virgin. But during turkey season, they can't think or talk about anything except turkey hunting. They forget to eat and sleep so that by the end of the first week, even the stoutest turkey hunter starts looking a little hollow. His grasp of basic concepts slips; his eyes go black and sunken. The deranged look would be enough, in itself, to scare normal people and children away. But turkey hunters are also incoherent: They speak in tongues. Sure, they can understand each other—but to everyone else, it's all just ravings from the asylum.

"First I laid a few little tree yelps on him and then I hit him with a fly-down cackle."

"Did he come off the roost?"

"Oh yeah, but he went right into full strut and hung up at a hundred yards."

"You cut at him?"

"And purred and cackled and yelped. But you know what finally worked?"

"You gobbled."

"That's right, brother. And he liked to run right over me." If that sounds like gibberish to you, then you're no turkey hunter. To me . . . well, it just sounds like the kind of phone conversation I have every night during turkey season. Hi, my name is Geoff, and I am one of the afflicted.

It hasn't always been that way—in fact, there was once a time when I was sane a full 12 months of the year. I knew a few turkey hunters when I was growing up, but there weren't as many turkeys back then—even in South Alabama—and the hunters who could find them were such extraordinary woodsmen that the craziness didn't matter. Who could argue with a person capable of calling a turkey into shotgun range with a hen's wingbone? But then the wild turkey began its astonishing comeback: from fewer than 20,000 just after the turn of the century, to some 4 million birds today. Where there had once been a few—like in South Alabama—there were suddenly a lot of turkeys. And in places where nobody had seen one for a couple of generations—like Vermont, where I've lived for 20 years—the bird was reestablished and quickly took hold. Craziness was breaking out all over.

All of a sudden, it seemed, anyone could learn to be a turkey hunter—even if they were really an accountant, say, or a carpenter. If you could lose your mind for one month of the year, you had potential. It turns out that several million Americans were well qualified.

For me, it started way back when with a springtime visit to Alabama. (Not only was I not crazy in those days, I had the good sense to leave Vermont during mud season.) A cousin of mine mentioned one night that turkey season would be opening soon and asked if I wanted to go out with him.

"Why not?" said I.

ANYONE CAN BE A TURKEY HUNTER: IF YOU CAN LOSE YOUR MIND FOR ONE MONTH OF THE YEAR, YOU HAVE POTENTIAL.

Amazing how casually we sometimes make decisions that change our lives: When I gave myself over to the turkey, I did it with a shrug.

I had to hustle around and find myself some camouflage clothes. I believe I even borrowed a shotgun since mine were packed away back in Vermont. I didn't bother to buy any calls since I didn't know how to use them; I figured I'd let my cousin do the calling. Turns out, he had something better in mind. He had lined up one of the best turkey hunters in the state to go along with me and show me how it was done. This fellow was so good, my cousin said, that he judged calling contests.

I made a sound to show how impressed I was—but actually I was thinking, "calling contests?" The notion seemed weird at the time; these days, I can tell you who won the National. I met my cousin and this man named Bill at the diner in town. The farmers weren't even up yet—everyone in the place was dressed in camouflage. Bill said we'd be covering some good ground. "I been hunting turkeys there for more than 40 years," he said. "Killed a few, too. Sure have."

I told him I'd never been turkey hunting.

"Well, if we get some action, you'll regret every morning when you weren't a turkey hunter."

Half an hour later, we parked under a live oak and walked down a logging road, through a stand of old longleaf. The air was cool and smelled of pine. Some light was gathering in the sky but the birds hadn't started yet. It was quiet and very still. Bill turned off the road and stopped where the ground began to slope down to a little creek bottom that was thick with gum. He told me to sit down, with my back against a big oak. I got set up. By now, I was hearing the first few tentative bird calls of the day.

Bill walked off a few steps, threw his head back and began speaking owl.

Who cooks for you? Who cooks for you?

Seeing a grown man standing out in the woods before dawn, hooting like an owl, made me wonder about Bill a little and—since I was sitting next to him—about myself more than a little. But then I heard my first gobble—a needy, aggressive blast. Bill hooted again, the turkey gobbled back and now I'm the fool with the wingbone in his mouth.

Bill, he purely loves calling turkeys. He used mouth yelpers, slates, box calls, and a wingbone. I believe he would have used a tuba if someone had convinced him it would do him some good. Our gobbler took his time flying down and was even more careful about coming in, so Bill got to use just about everything in his arsenal. He cackled, yelped, purred, and clucked. And the turkey gobbled and double-gobbled and, finally, came in to a little clear piece of ground in front of us, maybe 30 steps from where I was sitting. He spread out into full strut with his breast all puffed out and his tail fanned and the tips of his wings dragging the ground: magnificent.

I kept waiting for the bird to come a little closer—or maybe I was just enjoying the show and didn't want to end it by taking a shot. Whatever the reason, I waited a little too long. A deer came out of the thick trees along the creek, got a whiff of my breakfast sausage, and spooked. With a few frantic *put, put, put* calls, the turkey was right behind him. My hands were shaking.

Bill didn't seem to care—he was in it for the calling—and by that point, I didn't either. I had the fever. I wanted my first turkey to be

Crow or owl calls will often jump-start morning gobbling.

one I had called in myself. On the way out of the woods, I asked Bill some questions about calling. He told me to get started on a mouth yelper. He had a few extras back at the truck—he gave me one and told me how to fit it into the roof of my mouth and force air across the reed.

I almost gagged when I tried it. "Takes some getting used to. Practice and it'll come to you."

I started practicing in my own car, on the way back to the house, and I kept practicing every time I had to drive somewhere. I was stopped at a light one spring day, blowing a few off-key yelps, when I felt I was being watched. I turned and looked through my open window

and into the face of a woman who stopped next to me. A nicely dressed suburbanite, she gave me a look that said life was getting just too weird when you couldn't go to the hairdresser without some hollow-eyed, camouflaged lunatic making rutting boar noises in the next car. I thought about trying to explain but decided it was hopeless. She probably would have called the cops.

I went out every day for the rest of the season and I practiced my calling until I about drove my wife and kids out of the house. "Mom," I'd hear one of my daughters shout, "he's doing it again."

I wanted to be a good—nay, a great turkey caller—so I bought tapes and listened to them. I practiced on dozens of different calls: slates, boxes, diaphragms—anything that made it into the catalogues eventually wound up in my hands or in my mouth. I also got good turkey hunters like Bill to listen to me and tell me what I was doing wrong. Eventually, I even went to a couple of calling contests. For inspiration, I suppose.

But obsession is no substitute for talent and I never did become a very good caller. Not one who can converse with a gobbler for an hour and never make a mistake. (If I tried that, the gobbler would evacuate in the first 10 minutes.) Among turkey hunters, however, there seem to be two schools of thought about calling: one believes that less is more, the other holds that too much is not enough. After a few failures, I joined the minimalists. Now I call as little as I can get by with, and our house no longer sounds like a chicken coop because old Dad is upstairs working on his fly-down cackle. But you can be a minimalist caller—blow haiku poetry on your mouth yelper—and still be a turkey nut. I am, Lord help me, proof in the flesh.

After calling, I got into tactics in a big way. Lots of discussion about what to do when a gobbler is hanging up out of range. Do you shut up? Call more urgently? Move? Gobble? I burned up the phone lines discussing these issues with my fellow inmates. The Vermont season, which lasts a month, gave me lots of opportunity to experiment with tactics: We have hills and plenty of streams, so I got to test various theories about turkeys being unwilling to cross water and preferring to fly downhill off a roost and so forth. I also got to hunt in very different weather conditions. I shot one turkey in a snowstorm—a blizzard, actually—with the wind howling so loudly that I couldn't hear my own calls. And I have hunted innumerable mornings that were perfect in every respect save one . . . not one gobbler reared its head.

YOU CAN BE A MINIMAL CALLER— BLOW HAIKU POETRY ON YOUR MOUTH YELPER— AND STILL BE A TURKEY NUT.

Since I am fortunate enough to live a couple of miles from decent turkey woods, I'm free to indulge my obsession, limited only by the game laws and common sense. I actually do obey the law, but where turkeys are concerned I have no sense at all, common or otherwise: One season I went out 25 mornings after the same bird. The other 5 days, I was out of town and in agony, and on the fifth night—the eve of closing day—I caught the last plane home. I got in around 3:30, and woke my wife, who hadn't expected me: "Can you remember where I put my boots?"

"You're not going out now, are you?" she said, in bleary disbelief.

"Not unless I find my boots."

I worked the turkey for an hour that morning but he hung up at 100 yards and when I moved, he made me and bolted. In 26 mornings, I never did get a shot at him. That was a great season.

The next year wasn't so great. On the second day of the season, I got two turkeys with one shot. Pure luck, of the worst kind. I had limited-out and was through for the season. For the rest of May, I could sleep in. I felt the way a kid does, Christmas morning, when all the presents have been opened and it isn't even breakfast time yet.

During turkey season, you lose weight, lose sleep, and even lose your already feeble grip on lucidity. But you wish that it would never end. You just can't get enough. Turkey hunting is about as good an example of obsession as I am likely to come up with. No matter how strung out I am at the end of the season, I always wish it would last just a little longer. An Alabama turkey hunter once told me that his idea of paradise would be to follow the dogwoods right up the East Coast one spring.

"Didn't know you like flowers that much," I said.

"I like 'em enough," he replied. "But it isn't the flowers themselves. What I like about dogwoods is that, when they're blooming, the turkeys are gobbling. I'd like to start down in Florida in March and work my way up to New York toward the end of May. By then, I'd have had almost enough turkey hunting."

I've sort of appropriated that fantasy for myself. It is the turkey hunter's nirvana, a springtime that goes on and on: It is always dawn, with the first few birds calling for mates and some crows giving you hell as you slip down a logging road; in the thin, watery light, the dogwood blossoms look improbably white and pure; the air smells clean and you're full of eagerness and hope. It's spring, and as you strain to hear the season's first bird—with its own notes of madness—you think that of all the ways to go over the edge, this has to be the best.

⟫⬥⟪

LESSONS
FROM
THE BOSS

by Doug Harbour

HOW WELL HAVE YOU LEARNED YOUR LESSONS?
BECAUSE EVERY TIME YOU HUNT FOR TURKEYS, YOU
NEED TO REMEMBER WHAT HAPPENED TO YOU THE
LAST TIME YOU ENGAGED IN THIS PURSUIT.

A FEW YEARS AGO my father hunted with me in the juniper and piñion caverns of southern Colorado. We had worked a bird early in the morning that had whipped us. By midmorning we resorted to slowly moving down a cotton-wood creek bottom, setting up every half-mile in a good locale and calling, hoping to entice an old gobbler to answer.

We covered a couple of miles and stopped for about the fourth time. I laid down next to a gnarled juniper, and Dad planted his little camo folding stool into a clump of buck brush 10 yards to my left. I wasn't even carrying a gun. I wanted to watch the maestro in action!

Dad let out with a delicate yelp from his mouth call. Nothing. A minute later he cut loose with a real loud hen yelp. Instantly, above a sheer bluff across the creek, an old boss thundered back!

Dad eased his head around, and I could see a determined, conniving grin through his face mask. Hee, hee, hee—the duel was on!

A minute passed and Dad called again. The old monarch on the rim screamed back and then strutted into view. The tom would puff up for minutes on end, then strut back and forth on a rock pinnacle.

Time seemed to stand still as the duel raged. The sun worked its way westward, but neither adversary would give an inch. Finally, Dad whispered, "Hit him with your Lynch call. I want to try something."

I gave a loud *yelp, yelp, yelp*. Dad cut me off with a thunderous gobble. The old monarch far above went crazy. He double-gobbled, triple-gobbled and then pitched off the pinnacle and sailed straight toward us.

The king landed 60 yards slightly downhill. He instantly puffed up and marched to a strategic rise 40 yards away! He peered intently into Dad's clump of buck brush. He looked for "his" flirtatious girlfriend and her insolent lover.

Dad let out with a quiet seductive yelp. The old boss gobbler swung into action. He pranced straight to Dad!

I waited for the shot. At five feet the gobbler stopped and methodically examined every inch of the bush, looking for his girlfriend. I was afraid the old bird would spot my face mask being blown back and forth or hear my heart pounding in my chest. I marveled at how Dad could hold so still and seem so calm.

After an agonizing minute, the monarch turned and calmly strutted back up the rise. At 40 yards Dad yelped; the gobbler impatiently thundered and then turned and charged once more. At exactly five feet he again stopped and peered into Dad's bush.

This marvelous scenario repeated itself time after time. Maybe an hour passed or maybe it was a half-day. The old gobbler made countless trips to and from Dad. I witnessed a variety of sights and sounds that only an encounter of this magnitude could provide.

Boom! The roar of Dad's shotgun echoed through the canyon, and the spine-tingling duel was over. With one leg asleep and adrenaline pumping through my veins, I could barely stand up to congratulate my father.

Watching Dad play that gobbler like a violin taught me an awful lot. First, it doesn't matter what time of day you work a bird. If the gobbler's hormones are in high gear and he is "temporarily" out of girlfriends, he'll come to your call. Next, even though it is usually easier to successfully work a tom from about the same elevation, it is possible to pull a bird up or down a ridge or even across an obstacle such as a creek. The key is to have one heck of a lot of patience, confidence and willingness to experiment with your calls. Lastly, you don't have to pop the gobbler as soon as he gets into range.

Awhile back a friend and his wife hunted with me during the opening weekend of the spring season. Within the first hour Dave and I pulled in a big 21-pound gobbler, which Dave nailed. His wife, Glenda, and I hunted for the next couple of days and had some close encounters, but finally she had to go home skunked.

Two weeks before the next year's season she called and asked if she could come by herself, because she wanted to get a bigger gobbler than her hubby's. I grinned; Glenda had "turkey fever."

Just after sunup on the first morning, I spotted three long-bearded gobblers. They were feeding along a rise just above the almost-dry creek that meandered down the canyon. Through my spotting scope, they looked huge even at a mile. The terrain was perfectly suited for a stalk that would put us within good calling distance.

Glenda and I slipped into the steep-banked arroyo that the little creek had cut into the soft earth. The dirt bank was high enough that we didn't even have to stoop over as we quietly eased down to a position within 150 yards of the gobblers.

I crawled up behind a huge cottonwood and peeked over the rise. All three birds nonchalantly scratched and fed in a 30-yard opening. They were totally at ease and did not suspect a thing.

Keeping my hand below the bank, I motioned for Glenda to ease up behind the tree, too. Everything worked perfectly, and the birds continued to feed.

With my double-reed mouth call in place and a box call in my lap, I

let out the most seductive series of yelps I could muster. None of those long-bearded gobblers ever looked our way. In the next few minutes I cackled, *kee-keed* and tried every conceivable call without ever getting even the slightest reaction from any of the birds.

Totally frustrated, Glenda and I eased back down into the creek bed and slipped closer to the birds. When I peeked out this time, the sunlight sparkled on those gobblers, and they were only 60 yards away. *Hee, hee, hee,* I ought to be able to pull one of them 20 yards, I thought.

Once again I cut loose with a sexy yelp. Nothing. I tried a coarse, bossy call. Nothing. I tried every call imaginable in the next 15 minutes, and if anything, the gobblers moved a little farther away.

Finally, in desperation and indignation, I screamed the meanest, nastiest series of yelps possible. Instantly, on a ridge high above the valley floor, a faint gobble echoed back.

Ten seconds later a huge gobbler helicoptered into view and landed

20 yards on the other side of the three longbeards. He gobbled, then dropped his head and raced straight at us. I turned and whispered, "Shoot him when you can see him."

Glenda looked and whispered, "Oh you'd better see this!" By the time I had eased up to see, the boss gobbler was almost out of sight, sprinting a yard behind one of the longbeards! He chased him a mile down the creek bottom. In the 30-yard opening, one of the other subordinate gobblers flopped a couple of more times, then flew in the opposite direction up the creek. I never did see what had happened to the third bird.

We sat spellbound for a few minutes, as I tried to sort out all that had happened and attempted to form a new game plan. Finally, Glenda and I crawled along the edge of the opening to a little rise that overlooked the creek bottom in the direction the king had vanished.

On the crest of the rise there was a natural ambush site. In the center of four clumps of yucca was a sandy depression from which we could see almost a mile down the creek.

With loud, bossy calls I started yelping in earnest. Fifteen minutes later a black speck materialized against the gray-brown background. I focused my Bushnell spotting scope, and the king appeared in full strut.

HE HAD WHIPPED HIS SUBJECTS INTO TOTAL SUBMISSION BY HIS DOMINATION.

This boss of boss toms strutted almost nonstop until he was 40 yards away. Glenda lay prone with her shotgun against her shoulder and the barrel eased out through an opening in the yucca. I knew that when the old bird stepped into her view, he would be an easy shot.

All of a sudden, at 20 yards the gobbler casually veered to the right. I whispered to Glenda to stay absolutely flat and turn 180 degrees. I held her gun until she had made the switch.

Our adversary never spotted a thing. When he stepped in front of the gun barrel he dropped strut and stuck his head straight up. *Boom!*

The king was down. That majestic bird, when he folded, never even flopped or spread his fan.

Glenda's gobbler not only provided us with a rare perspective on visually working birds from start to finish, but also back at camp, he outweighed her husband's bird by a full pound.

I concluded in the aftermath of this fantastic duel that many of the theories that I had read and heard from turkey biologists are true. Glenda's bird was definitely the king of his valley. He had whipped his subjects into total submission by his domination. If another gobbler showed the slightest interest in a hen, the fight was on.

The experts say that on a perfectly still and quiet morning only one-quarter of the gobblers in an area will sound off. The rest have been intimidated to the point where they won't make a peep—much less a gobble. It reminds me of Marine Corps boot camp: a gunnery sergeant glaring at his new recruits.

Last spring, a young tom taught me a true lesson in humility and gave me an insight into a turkey's mental capabilities. The story is, however, a little embarrassing.

The chamber of commerce from El Dorado, Kansas, invited me to participate in the Governor's Annual One Shot Turkey Hunt. I strutted around my house gathering my gear and secretly grinning as I considered my competition—pro bass fishermen, country-western singers and other noted experts in their non-turkey-hunting fields.

Before daylight on that fateful morning, my guide, Dennis, and I were hunkered down with our backs against a couple of big trees waiting for the first gobbler to sound off. The wind was blowing, and I was a little edgy, but it was reassuring to know that the day before my partner had seen five gobblers working the field that lay 20 yards away in the inky darkness.

Finally, 10 minutes before sunup we heard a faint gobble cutting through the wind. It came from the edge of a field that bordered ours, 300 yards away. I got my calls out and started working.

An hour passed, and even though we could still occasionally coax a whispering reply to our overtures, the gobblers remained in the far field. It was apparent that our tactics needed to be revamped.

Dennis and I crawled on our bellies for 150 yards until we edged up to the border of the gobblers' domain. I left my partner, and using a tree stump to block my approach, I crawled another 15 yards to where I could see the panorama. Peeking out, I watched a flock of eight turkeys scratching, strutting and carrying on.

I started to call *yelp, yelp, yelp, yelp.* The birds were very interested in each other, but were only vaguely concerned about this new seductive temptress calling from the edge of their field.

Suddenly, the birds' behavior took a bizarre turn. Three of them ran 50 yards to the right while the others tore around in the open field, doing figure-eights. Then they all ran to the middle of the field.

I yelped, and three birds immediately flushed! While the airborne birds flew toward the creek bottom, the others ran like greyhounds straight at me.

At 50 yards I could see that each of the five birds had beards two or three inches long. I had to make a decision—they were jakes, but the wind was really howling!

The teenagers came to a screeching stop, for just a second, at an opening in the fence at 20 paces. I put the bead on the biggest one's red head.

Boom! The bird went down and then jumped up and flushed into the air. I shot again, and the ends of a couple of tail feathers blew back toward me as the gobbler sailed off!

I was sick! I had wounded the bird. Sadly, my hard-working partner and I examined, on our hands and knees, every square inch of the ground where the gobbler was standing when I shot first.

We couldn't find a drop of blood or even a cut little neck feather. Apparently, just as I fired, the bird had naturally stumbled, and my shot had missed. I was fairly certain that only the leading edge of my pattern of No. 6 shot had cut the tail feathers.

Sheepishly, I mumbled an apology to Dennis, because I knew how much the governor's hunt meant to him. Moving off in the direction the jake had sailed, I kept trying to kick myself in the seat of my pants.

A quarter-mile down the creek bank we sat down on an old log to plan our strategy. It was mutually decided to just sit still and quiet. Maybe if one of those No. 6s found its mark, we would hear the bird flopping in one of the brushy thickets down the creek. Perhaps, too,

Mother Nature might intervene and grant us some other reprieve.

An hour later, we dejectedly decided to quit the spooked creek bottom and head to another drainage. I stood up, took about 10 steps and heard *gobble, gobble.*

The old tom sounded as if he was calling from my hip pocket. He was directly upwind, and *close.* Dennis eased to the ground, and I crawled up a steep bank where I could have a field of fire.

Peeking through last year's thick, dead grass, I spotted the gobbler in the mouth of a feeder draw 70 yards away. Lying flat, I slipped in my mouth call and eased my shotgun straight out in front.

With my neck stretched at an awkward angle so that I could watch the show, I cut loose with a series of yelps. Before the second note reached the tom, he wheeled and pointed that red-headed periscope straight toward me.

Gobble, gobble, gobble. The lovesick tom screamed his passion. He then raced along the base of the hill until he was right in front of my gun barrel—40 yards away.

I gave a quiet series of yelps. The tom puffed up and started in. The alert red head bobbed with each step closer. At 15 yards I put the bead on that warty red head and squeezed the trigger.

Dennis and I ran up and examined that beautiful bird. I was amazed to see a little jake beard, and low and behold, three of the tail feathers had recently been cut. This young tom had to be the same bird that I had shot at an hour earlier.

That young bird taught me that a gobbler is sometimes given a little too much credit for his mental capabilities. Even though a wild turkey possesses an amazing ability to pinpoint exactly where a call is originating, and its tremendous eyesight will detect the slightest movement, it does not necessarily have the ability to remember what happened even an hour before.

Of all the lessons that lovesick gobblers have provided, the most important was provided by this jake. He taught me that the majesty of the duel is all-encompassing—especially when I had to tell the story of my "three shot jake" at the banquet for the Annual Kansas Governor's One Shot Turkey Hunt.

THE
OLD MAN
AND
THE TOM

by Charles Elliot

**I'D SEEN MORE THAN 60 TURKEY
HUNTING SEASONS COME AND GO.
OLD AGE HAD TAKEN ITS TOLL, YET I STILL FELT
COMPELLED TO ANSWER THE GOBBLES OF SPRING.**

Although Charlie Elliott has been an Outdoor Life *editor for more
years than he probably cares to remember, this article may have
been the most difficult to write. Long before there were such things
as "turkey-hunting experts," there was Charlie Elliott. Charlie
remains the acknowledged "grandfather of modern-day turkey
hunting." Few writers have influenced their audience more than*

Charlie. When he once mentioned in a story that slamming his car door had coerced a tom into gobbling, hunters around the country followed suit in an effort to locate their spring bird.

Charlie offered readers much more conservative turkey hunting information as well. Turkeys, turkey hunters and the times have surely changed, but at more than 80 years old, Charlie Elliott can still do what he did best: hunt gobblers and write about them. We'd like to share a letter from Charlie with you. This note was written to Executive Editor Vin T. Sparano and helps capture the spirit of one of the best outdoor writers in the business.

Dear Vin,

I finally dug my spurs in and wrote this turkey piece we talked about. I'm just about now getting back on my feet from that siege I had with the medics more than a year ago. I feel better than I have in a long time. For a while there I was afraid I'd live—I feel good enough now to be afraid I won't. I figure I should be well on the way to reasonably good shape for an old hunter. On the other hand, I guess I'll end up like I told Polly the other day—probably the last thing I'll ever do is crawl across my office floor, reach up and hit the wrong key on the typewriter.

If he lives alone, or lives long enough, an outdoorsman is likely to arrive at a certain stage of life when he begins to talk to himself. Whether he's lonely, or beyond his allotted span, or has slipped a cog in the upper story, thinking out loud seems to help solve whatever problem he has at hand.

At the moment, though, there was no mite of satisfaction in the castigation I was heaping upon myself.

"You're an old fool. Your eyes won't let you see an ostrich if one stepped on your toes. You couldn't hear a jet plane if it flew close enough to knock off your face mask. You have hardly enough lung capacity to blow your nose, and your legs get wobbly if you walk to the mailbox. By what stretch of the imagination do you think you can hear, call up, see and bag a wild turkey gobbler?"

It really wasn't that bad, but it was the way I felt at the moment. Yet, there I was, perched on a mountain slope in turkey woods, trying to recapture some of the golden moments of other years when my senses were strung like a tight bow string.

For more than 60 years, few seasons had come and gone that I didn't bring home one or more gobblers. Two years ago, that special utopia suddenly became a thing of the past when old age caught up with me and I fell on hard physical times. For months, my medical insurer and I kept a couple of hospitals in business and provided several medical men with good vacations. Somehow, my 80-plus-year-old hide and carcass inside it survived the cutting and chemicals, but I had lost more than my share of turkey hunting days.

At the opening of this new gobbler season, I was a long call from being loaded with vim and vigor, as I had been in other days not too far behind me. I had not lost my awareness of how necessary it is for a man to have his senses sharp and working if he expects to compete with an old-feathered Einstein.

With me were two companions whom I considered among the most knowledgeable turkey hunters in the country. I had hunted with each over many seasons. Roscoe Reams has been a regular companion for more than 40 years, and we've shared many splendid hours in the woods. My other partner, Frank Piper, is on my list of most favorite Yankees. He owns and operates Penn's Woods Products, a national manufacturer of calls and other turkey hunting equipment.

Each of these hunting mates had been thoughtful enough to pull me aside and privately propose that because my physical equipment was not up to par, he go along as my eyes and ears and call my bird close enough for me to see and shoot.

THE FIRST GOBBLER I EVER BAGGED WAS FROM THIS REGION IN 1923.

To each proposal, I explained: "I really appreciate this, but it won't be the same unless I do it on my own. Maybe I can find a bearded one as retarded and decrepit as I am."

They had respected my wish, gone up another trail and left this neck of the mountain to me.

We were smack in the middle of one of those mysterious periods that tom turkeys go through without gobbling. The mating season may be in full swing, the temperature perfect, the barometer high, the birds known to strut and the hens to go to them, but sometimes when every condition seems perfect, the gobblers clam up for a few days for no apparent reason.

The first two mornings of the season, I left the high country to my partners and devoted my efforts to the lower ridges around the little valley. I called and listened from a half-dozen points that I could climb without splitting my spleen but heard no gobbling. Higher on the mountain, both Frank and Roscoe saw turkeys feeding but could get no vocal response from the birds.

"Because there is no way I can keep up with you jackalopes on these mountain slopes," I told them at lunch on the second day, "I'll follow the next best procedure I know—calling, waiting and hoping."

The first gobbler I ever bagged was from this region in 1923, and over the years of hunting since then, I was well-acquainted with the territory. Around Roscoe's camp, I knew those coves in which the birds fed regularly. Also pinpointed were several roost sites where we never failed to find birds early in the season.

Because my climbing was limited, my best bet was to set up shop along one of the most popular travel routes between the dinner table and bedroom limbs and call just enough to interest some gobbler with a craw full of curiosity.

I could only guess how the turkeys felt about it, but I thought that the spot I had selected was ideal. I arranged my blind in the edge of open hardwoods along a small creek. If the torn earth was any indication, several large coves on both sides of the creek below must have been abundant with acorns, grubs and other choice tidbits of a turkey's diet. The feeding area channeled into a narrow passageway along the creek to the roost site on the ridge.

For most of my turkey hunting life, I constructed my blinds out of dead tree limbs, brush, live foliage or whatever material I happened to find on the spot that could be arranged to break my outline. In the past three or four years, I have found it much less time-consuming to carry a camouflage net blind, arranged on lightweight stakes that can be easily shoved into the soft earth to hide my body so that only my head shows. This gives me the opportunity to shift my legs or buttocks when they grow numb and painful from long waiting in an exposed position. The cloth blind hides the lower part of my anatomy more effectively because I tend toward the wiggle-worm type.

If you use your eyes, ears and a little bug juice in the proper places, a most delightful period that anyone can spend is sitting quietly in the woods, watching the endless play of drama and comedy of the wild citizens around you. The anticipation of hearing or seeing an old longbeard at any moment adds suspense to the sights and sounds of small birds moving through the trees with the muted music of a creek in the background.

All of this was pleasant, the afternoon was warm and I struggled to overcome the usual routine of an after-lunch nap in my favorite easy chair at home.

"Patience," I kept repeating. "Have patience. It's a turkey hunter's most useful asset."

Old age, or the nap habit, prevailed. For how long I don't know, but I opened my eyes suddenly. Either instinct or a lifetime of training kept me from moving my head. Seven hens and a small gobbler scratched the open woods in front of me. The jake seemed to be the only one of the flock curious about my blind. He moved cautiously toward it, a step or two at a time, and once he might have been within range, but with my poor depth perception I wasn't sure, so I didn't try him.

When the flock scratched on across the open woods and out of sight, I clucked softly, waited a few minutes, then yelped. There was no answer, but soon the hens and jake came back. When it appeared that they would again feed by, out of range, I tried another tactic. I gave what I considered a reasonable imitation of the *burr-rr-rr-r* call, used when the birds seem to greet or talk with one another. This got the flock's attention. Heads went up, and then it seemed that the entire group was talking. The birds didn't come any closer to my blind, but went slowly on up the creek, *burr-rr-rr-ring* and clucking to one another in a conversational tone, known to the mountaineers as *cacking*. When a flock carries on in this manner, it is an indication that the birds are undisturbed and at ease.

It was a nice show, a sort of rerun from other days, and I enjoyed it with no sense of disappointment that I had not tried the young gobbler at a questionable range.

I settled down with my back to the tree, watched and listened for a while and dozed again. One of the special quirks of an otherwise normal turkey hunter is that all of the rest of his body can go sound asleep in a turkey blind, but his ears never do. They filter out the usual forest sounds and file them away as unimportant, but any noise that could possibly be made by a turkey rings an alarm in his brain.

How long I slept, I do not know. A cluck woke me. A large gobbler came into focus, and I sat motionless while he walked slowly out of range. I was somewhat surprised that he was moving downstream, away from the roost site on the mountain. But he seemed in no way disturbed.

When he was out of sight, I clucked a couple of times. A few minutes later, I yelped softly. I followed this after a short interval with a series of lusty yelps. For more minutes, I strained for an answer that never came. More in frustration than in hope, I gobbled the box like an old tom turkey mad at the world. The only result was the derisive caw of a crow down by the creek.

My inclination of the moment was to give it up and walk to camp, but, once more, I told myself: "Patience! Have patience, like you advise everyone else. You're in a good location. You've seen turkeys. Stay put!"

I didn't call any more. There are two schools of thought on calling. One says that you should continue to cluck and yelp to attract any bird passing by. The other school, to which I belong, thinks that once a turkey has you pinpointed, he will eventually arrive to investigate.

That must be the only reason that kept the seat of my pants compatible with the roots, rocks and contour of the ground under the tree against which I sat.

I take no credit for character. In spite of all of this, I was on the very verge of standing up, gathering my gear and taking the trail to that bourbon and branch water when the gobbler that had strolled by less than an hour earlier was suddenly in front of me. Without making a sound, he had sneaked back, apparently looking for the source of my calls.

He walked very slowly, but every movement showed how alert he was. When his eye disappeared behind a tree trunk, I put the gun to my shoulder and when he appeared again, my sights were on his neck. I held them there until he paused suddenly, almost in the middle of a stride, his head high and suspicious. Praying that my judgment of distance was correct and that he was within range, I squeezed off a shot.

The gobbler half-fell on his side, then regained his balance and roared upward on wings that carried him at an angle across the slope. He was in the trees before I could get off another shot. I stumbled over the edge of the blind and ran a few steps to get a line on the course of his flight, but he was out of sight. I stood still and listened for him to crash or to hear his dying flutter but heard nothing.

I knew that the bird had been hit hard because I found neck feathers where he had stood when I shot. For more than an hour, I combed that mountain slope in the direction the bird had flown. I climbed to look at limbs or piles of debris that might have been my turkey. I looked under logs, around laurel thickets, but not a feather could I find. Heartsick to the core at wounding such a magnificent bird, I took the trail to camp.

I was glad to find that Roscoe had come in early. I gave him a blow-by-blow of my unhappy experience.

"We've got about 30 minutes of daylight left," I suggested. "Why don't you carry your eyes back up there with me for a last look?"

"I was hoping you'd ask," Roscoe said.

We were on the trail about 150 yards from where I shot when Roscoe commented casually, "I know what happened to your bird."

"Wh-what?" I stammered. "What?"

He made no reply but walked on ahead of me for 40 yards and picked up my gobbler. It was lying beside the trail but in such a position in the leaves that with my defective eyesight I'm sure I never would have seen it.

Weighed on the scales in Roscoe's cabin, the gobbler was a 20-pounder. It sported a slightly more than nine-inch beard.

"Well," I said, "that does it. I'm just too damned old and infirm to hunt gobblers anymore."

Roscoe grinned.

"We've got one more day here," he said. "You've taken only half of your season limit. What time do you think we should get up in the morning?"

Credits

Photographers

Jon Blumb
Lawrence, KS

© Jon Blumb: p. 115

Toby Bridges
Pearl, IL

© Toby Bridges: p. 120

Gary W. Griffen
Red Hook, NY

© Gary W. Griffen: pp. 9T, 36, 98, 154-155, 164

Donald M. Jones
Troy, MT

© Donald M. Jones: pp. 10B, 26-27, 62-63, 86BL, 87T, 109, 204-205

Lance Krueger
McAllen, TX

© Lance Krueger: pp. 4, 10T, 17, 70, 103, 182

Wyman Meinzer
Benjamin, TX

© Wyman Meinzer: pp. 86BR, 87B, 198

Larry Mueller
St. Jacob, IL

© Larry Mueller: p. 170

Jeff Murray
Duluth, MN

© Jeff Murray: p. 148

Martin J. Tarby
Rapid City, SD

© Martin J. Tarby: p. 110

Lovett Williams
Cedar Key, FL

© Lovett Williams: pp. 9B, 19, 86T

Jim Zumbo
Cody, WY

© Jim Zumbo: p. 131

Illustrators

Stephen Fadden
Harleysville, PA

© Stephen Fadden: p. 180

Clay McGaughy

© Clay McGaughy: pp. 210-211, 220-221

Arnold Roth
New York, NY

© Arnold Roth: p. 136

Michael Schumacher

© Michael Schumacher: pp. 55, 57

Steve Stankiewicz
New York, NY

© Steve Stankiewicz: p. 105 all

Larry Zach
Ankeny, IA

© Larry Zach: cover

(Note: T=Top, C=Center, B=Bottom, L=Left, R=Right, I=Inset)